Dearest MaRiky

All proceeds from the sale of this book will go to the Riky Rick Foundation for the Promotion of Artivism.

First published by Jacana Media (Pty) Ltd in 2023

10 Orange Street
Sunnyside
Auckland Park, 2092
South Africa
+2711 628 3200
www.jacana.co.za

© Louisa Zondo, 2023

All rights reserved.

ISBN 978-1-4314-3293-6

Cover design by Megan Mance
Editing by Rehana Rossouw
Proofreading by Lara Jacob
Set in Ehrhardt 12/15pt
Printed and bound by ABC Press, Cape Town
Job no. 004021

See a complete list of Jacana titles at www.jacana.co.za

Praise for *Dearest MaRiky*

'An individual journey that while very different from that of most people in South Africa will resonate with many.'
Koketso Moeti, executive director of Amandla.mobi and chairperson of the SOS Coalition

'Louisa invites you to the depth of her pain yet manages to leave you hopeful. A book for everyone, men and women, young and old.'
Sibongile Mkhabela, CEO of Barloworld Empowerment Foundation and trustee at Trust Africa

'She courageously and compassionately breaks the silence of her own, her son's and our country's traumas – may it help us as we navigate deeply interwoven personal and political trauma.'
Pregs Govender, writer, activist and author of Love and Courage: A story of insubordination

'An emotional yet powerful account of a mother's journey through the grief of a son's death by suicide and self-rediscovery by excavating buried wounds towards healing and service to her son's community of fans.'
Simamkele Dlakavu, African feminist activist, researcher, writer, and communication and sustainability professional

'"And Still I Rise" is what I thought after reading it as some of the hardships are brutal and defeating. Louisa is very brave and strong and yet also very fragile. A very real illustration of life for black women in South Africa.'
Zanele Monnakgotla, non-executive director for Ecobank Transnational Incorporated, Rand Water and the Small Enterprise Development Agency

'[This book] is an invitation to all of us to revisit our stories and places of woundedness and to trust that divine love – God – will meet us there. It is always enough. We are enough.'
'This book is a must read.'
Penny Moumakwa, CEO and founder of Mohau Equity Partners, a medical doctor and former executive director at Discovery Health and EXCO member of Discovery Holdings

'The honesty with which she describes the many painful aspects of her life allows all who read it to recognise themselves in different aspects of her story. This book is a perfect gift for people at multiple stages in their lives and will be a lifeline to many.'
Reverend Nontombi Naomi Tutu, speaker, advocate, educator

'[…] healing is a lifelong intentional journey. It is not a destination or a problem we need to solve.'
Lulu Gwagwa, founder of Traversing Liminality and Mhakazi Trust, chairperson of Barloworld Ltd and the Firstrand Foundation, and CEO of Lereko Investments (Pty) Ltd

'Louisa's honesty, vulnerability and compassion make this book a must read for anyone seeking understanding and hope in the face of tragedy.'
Charlotte McClain, Global Disability Advisor for the World Bank Group and a global thought leader on disability rights and inclusion

'*Dearest MaRiky* is a deeply resonant memoir for anyone who has ever been loved, wounded, violated, ashamed, lost, found, healed and liberated.'
Lwando Xaso, constitutional lawyer, writer, historian; trustee of the Constitutional Court Trust and founder of Including Society

'You craft each of your characters with compassion and understanding.'
Noel Daniels, CEO of Cornerstone Institute, non-executive director at the Cape Cultural Collective and Chairperson of Darkroom Contemporary Dance Theatre

'But above all, this story is about one woman's search for healing and wholeness in the aftermath of a family tragedy that forces her to reassess her own life and face up to the past.'
Eilidh Whiteford, former Scottish National Party (SNP) Member of Parliament, who served as SNP spokesperson for Women; Fishing, Food and Rural Affairs; and International Development

'Reading this book is not easy; a sadness rests upon it. Even so, it is a sort of love story that brims with healing possibilities. [It is] one that commits us all "to encounter all people with compassion".'
André Keet, Research Chair for Critical Studies in Higher Education Transformation and Deputy Vice Chancellor for Engagement and Transformation at Nelson Mandela University

'As a parting shot, the author suggests the mantra: "Leave a little space in your heart for the next person" by bringing compassion to all your interactions.'
Kefilwe Manana, writer, communications expert and reputation management specialist

'This book breaks the rules – it breaks the rules on silence, breaks the silence on suicide, GBV and grief. It sheds light on the quiet suffering and trauma that is harboured deep within the innermost fibres of our beings.'
Zen Mathe, investigator at Open Secrets and one of the authors of The Unaccountables

'Our lives are sacred. Ordinary, messy and sacred. The same applies to the telling of our life stories as Louisa Zondo has here, navigating how, what and when to tell – as an act of deep listening and trust. [...] We are worthy and capable of finding a new sense of wholeness through all this breaking. Louisa knows this.'
Malika Ndlovu, applied arts practitioner, poet and author of Invisible Earthquake: A woman's journal through stillbirth

Dearest MaRiky

A mother's journey through trauma, grief and healing

Louisa Zondo

My son, Rikhado 'Riky Rick' Makhado who, in his death, continues to whisper love and life into us.

My family and friends whose loving kindness and support have awakened me to the realisation that we are bound together in this journey of life, a journey that amazingly reveals its course as we travel it. I am grateful for your presence.

Every woman, as we struggle to reclaim our lives from the bludgeoning of gender-based violence, femicide and traumas of being woman.

I offer a word of solidarity and dedication to all who have lost loved ones from traumatic circumstances. We are, it seems, left with no choice but to walk spiritually alongside our loved ones and embrace the possibility that in continuing to live life with purpose, we might honour them.

'The business of coming home again is a dreadful exercise if you are a native. We used to be called "natives" when I was young here. And correctly. Now I find people are called blacks or whites or browns. Why?'

NONI JABAVU, *A STRANGER AT HOME*

'Forgiveness is to let go of our hope for a different or better past.'

RICHARD ROHR, *BREATHING UNDERWATER*

Contents

Preface	1
On the mountain	5
In the beginning	21
The Secret Pals	47
The Turfloop upheaval	61
Young mother, young student	69
Rikhado	77
A watershed	81
London calling	85
Home	89
The Constitution: The honouring of the experience of life	101
Cape Town blessings	111
Love and the cataclysm	115
Family values	127
Nothing else to offer	141
Postscript: We are not what has been done to us	155
Acknowledgements	161
Photo captions	163

Preface

On 23 February 2022 my second-born son, hip-hop artist Rikhado 'Riky Rick' Makhado, died from suicide, shattering my life. As I grappled to make sense of what living had become, I sought guidance and support in spiritual practice and committed myself to being of service to others through public speaking about the grief and trauma of losing my beloved son. I participated in several discussions raising awareness about the tragedy of suicide and maintaining wellness.

I went on an expedition to Mount Everest Base Camp twenty-five days after my son's death. The mountains wrapped me up in the softest blanket, clearing the path for me to decide to build on Rikhado's legacy of loving and caring for others, especially young people. However, when I returned from the mountain after two weeks, I realised that I was still deeply affected – almost immobilised – by sadness. This thoroughly confused and surprised me. Even as I spoke on public platforms about suicide, mental health and living through grief and trauma, I remained defeated and unable to cope.

In June 2022 I began therapy sessions with a psychologist. My life partner, Kumi Naidoo, and I sought joint counselling to deal with the grief of our son's death and work through the challenges in our relationship. Therapy was hard but we stuck with it. In time we both looked forward to our weekly sessions, which provided a safe space for us to address our thoughts and feelings, and to have the hard conversations that were impossible without guidance. Three months into our therapy sessions, I recovered a suppressed memory of a traumatic attack that had taken place after my thirty-fourth birthday.

My story is fifty-nine years old, and it is time for it to retire. It no longer serves me to be disconnected from myself and others, pleasing other people in a quest to be loved and valued, grappling with doubt and dishonouring myself. Writing this book was an opportunity to dredge the depths of my being to pull my story out, experience the pain of excavating it, attach words to it for the first time and observe the sensations in my entire being – body, mind and soul – as it was released. I learned hard lessons and sat with the emotions it brought up – including laughter, regret, pride, joy, gratitude, guilt, love and sadness – as I allowed the words to become a burial ceremony for the traumas of my past. As the emotions poured out of me, I was able to feel grateful for many aspects of my life.

Writing this book was my way of opening space for a new story to emerge and revitalise my life. I now hold the loss of my son in every breathing moment alongside gratitude for the opportunity I have to live life with renewed vitality. I am able now to gently embrace the moments when I am overcome by sadness and other emotions associated with my grief and trauma.

While my tale is similar to those many others could tell, I am hoping that it inspires others to avail themselves of the gifts of releasing the past and learning useful lessons from them. My experience of attempting to write this story before it was ready to come out urges me to warn those journeying through trauma and grief to be aware of the harm they may expose themselves to if they bring out pain that their minds and bodies might not be ready to confront. Being in circles of care – in whatever form or shape –

where it is safe to discuss trauma and grief, is vitally important to contain the risks of re-traumatising or sinking deep into the abyss of grief.

Now that I have written my story, I hope that it inspires me to live up to my commitment to encounter all people with compassion, in all circumstances. I continue to receive immeasurable compassion and loving kindness from family and friends even though, over the years, they suffered from my trauma-based irrational decisions. This heightens my awareness of the reality that I do not know what others are dealing with and therefore my best contribution to them must be to treat everyone with compassion all the time. My story teaches me that we all are doing the best we can with the capacities we have, and therefore even as we mess up in life (as I did), we all deserve compassion. This compassion may give space to someone caught up in a rage that may be associated with an unresolved trauma to navigate out of their flooding of emotion and perhaps address the root cause of their anger.

The experience of being stuck in a story, struggling to find ways of letting it go and seizing an opportunity for a new one to take root – enriched by key lessons from the past – seems to be the tale of the universe. Humanity is stuck in the stories of decayed political, economic, social, cultural and environmental systems, which perpetuate the violence and unsustainability of coloniality, misogyny, racism and greed. It seems that frameworks proposed as alternatives to the decayed systems replicate the violence and unsustainability and therefore do not contribute to the dismantling of oppression. It is encouraging, however, to observe the increasing discourse and enquiries about ways of learning lessons from the decayed systems and being open and realistic about the pain and discomfort it will take to put them to rest while investigating how communities in their many differentiated ways can cultivate new ways of being and doing.

As the discourse on the vision of humanity's participation in life as part of nature and connected to all of it deepens in all fields of human endeavour – including arts and culture, indigenous peoples and holders of ancient wisdoms, the economy, the environment, politics, social and natural sciences, activism and philanthropy – it is clear that the time has come for the decayed systems to die a natural death. Humanity needs to learn how to cultivate pathways that counter the legacies of a past stained by injustices. I see this as the emergence of humanity's new story. I look forward to my continued participation in a range of dialogues and to sitting in circles exploring ways of bringing humanity's new story to life.

MaRiky taught us a significant lesson about the role of arts and culture in touching the hearts and minds of people and bringing them to act on the changes they wish to see in their lives and in the world. Through the Riky Rick Foundation for the Promotion of Artivism, we hope to contribute to bringing together the worlds of arts, culture and activism ("artivism") and to inspire the participation of all in addressing humanity's horrendously difficult challenges. While acknowledging that no single pathway, including artivism, can address all the challenges, studies in the fields of neuroscience and psychology confirm the pivotal role of arts and culture in the development of neuro pathways which align with connectedness and the valuing of all life. Thank you MaRiky for leaving this learning and legacy for us to build on.

On the mountain

23 March 2022

Dearest MaRiky,

It's the early hours of the morning – 1.03am Nepali time, to be exact. It's been one month now, since 23 February 2022. The day on which your spirit and body separated. I am lying on my back in a warm bed in the Buddha Lodge, Phakding, Nepal. I'm in Nepal, because I am on my way walking to Mount Everest Base Camp, MaRiky. I'm awake at this hour because I'm reflecting on life, death and the meaning of everything. Since your death last month, I've been starkly aware of the need in me to make sense of where I am and how I am called to be. I decided to proceed with this trek to Mount Everest Base Camp. Not only because I knew you would want me to, but also because I imagined it would present the perfect opportunity, over fourteen days, for me to wrestle with the questions...

What is the moment?

How does this moment call me to be?

I am unskilled at staying with an enquiry – any enquiry – and going deep into it. You know this, because during your thirty-four years of life on this side, you watched me 'busy-body' myself through many crises. In fact, you were the first person to really teach me to sit with challenges and 'encounter them' without rushing to offer what I perceived to be solutions, without needing to wipe away the challenge. For this reason, my Mount Everest Base Camp walk will be embodied in a long conversation with you. I imagine that the conversation will not be neat and orderly. Little is clear to me. The conversation might just present itself as and when it emerges.

Little is clear to me, but I will proceed.

I will proceed, and I will open myself up to this moment and how it calls me to be...

24 March 2022

Dear MaRiky,

The experience of yesterday was beautiful. It was Day 2 of our Mount Everest Base Camp trek. Aunt Xoli and I walked with our trekking team after connecting with them on Monday evening, 22 March. We left Phakding at about 9am and headed for Namche Bazaar. It was a nine-hour trek filled with laughter, camaraderie, silence and physical anguish of the body. We ascended from 2 600m to 3 440m. I feel enormous gratitude that all of us in the team ended the day in high spirits and eager to treat our exhausted bodies to some much-deserved rest.

As I took in the unspeakable wonders of the mountain, the sense of you being part of it all was so real, MaRiky... I laughed out loud and shouted your name.

I still hold this huge awareness of your presence. It brings up an inexplicable warmth and softness in me. Being like this evokes the unforgettable feeling when gazing at a feeding baby in utter love. When baby returns the gaze with a coo, as milk trickles down the side of their mouth ... that primal feeding instinct. Such moments were, for me, always whispers of God's presence... Love's presence.

As I embraced your presence and connected with you, the middle stanza of Rumi's thirteenth-century poem 'A Great Wagon' came to me. That wisdom captured the essence of it all.

> Out beyond ideas of wrongdoing and rightdoing,
> there is a field. I'll meet you there.
> When the soul lies down in that grass,
> the world is too full to talk about.
> Ideas, language, even the phrase 'each other'
> doesn't make any sense.

Even as I stayed in the beauty, joy and peace of being connected with you, I saw the drastic erosion of this beautiful, majestic Himalayan mountain range. I saw the desperation of the custodians of the land as they grapple with the tyrannical demands of the tourism industry. They are being forced to cut down trees in order to upgrade their infrastructure to meet the insatiable needs of so-called 'paying tourists'. I saw – with great anger – the effects of corruption, which has caused many folk operating in the tourism industry to lose hope of ever recovering from the effects of the COVID-19 pandemic. I started wondering how you hold awareness of these and a plethora of other intersecting challenges.

Maybe one of the things you would do is to deepen understanding of how communities organise and seek to define and shape the meaningfulness of life for themselves.

Maybe I must explore this further…

24 March 2022

Dear MaRiky,

Today is Day 5 of the team's trek, and Day 4 for Aunty Xoli and me. We had an 'active' rest day, which saw us walk slowly for three and a half hours to the Everest Viewing Hotel 3 880m above sea level.

From the restaurant deck, we were able to get a glimpse of the summit of Mount Everest. This was a brief window of opportunity, as the mountain-top soon became completely cloaked in clouds. How exhilarating!

We encountered incredibly scenic landscapes,

yaks silently grazing, throughout the mountainous terrain. My heart was filled with joy.

I recalled your enormous warmth. Reels of videos capturing your playful soul came to mind, as I absorbed the serenity of the moment. MaRiky, the breathtaking beauty of this mountain is laced with stark contrasts and contradictions of deep-rooted hardship, toil and exploitation. Experiencing these reminds me of how your life continuously taught me to hold in awe both the great joys of life and the devastating harms of our existence.

It brought into focus a thought shared by James Finley in a lecture I heard many years ago on Transforming Trauma. It goes something like, 'You know that you love someone when you have had a glimpse of something so beautiful in them, that it can never die.'

It's blissful to realise that your life gave real meaning to this wisdom. I am grateful to this Mount Everest Base Camp trek for presenting me with this insight.

You remain immense beauty, MaRiky. I joyfully confirm that, to me, you can never die.

I love you to infinity, MaRiky.
Mama

25 March 2022

Dear MaRiky,

Our trek has brought us to Lobuche. This is Day 5 of our trek. On today's walk, we gained some elevation and reached one of the oldest monasteries in Nepal, at 3 700m, then descended to 3 400m to sleep low at the Paradise Lounge and Restaurant in Lobuche.

Internet connectivity is rather weak at this point, and I may not be able to transmit this message. We will certainly have no connectivity over the next two days in Tengboche, so the posting of my musings on those days will be delayed until connectivity is established. Today's seven-hour trek was filled with richness. We got the opportunity, once again, to observe Mount Everest.

As we continued to trek upwards, for two and a half hours on a truly steep trail, it occurred to me that while Mount Everest is the highest of all peaks in the world, from where we were, it appeared lower than the other peaks in the Himalayan range. This is a matter of perspective and it led me to consider how I have so often acted on what I perceive with my physical senses – as if it was the only and absolute truth. I thought how easily I go about life blinded to perspective. As is characteristic of the mind, this led to thinking on numerous areas, including mental health.

Your death, MaRiky, was met with deep shock, pain and sadness internationally. It ignited wide discussion about depression and mental illness in general. As I thought about the range of traumas that affect our mental health, I found myself reviewing ways in which society is experiencing collective traumas. Thoughts about the violence of misogyny, racism, corruption, greed, poverty, inequality and other injustices brought darkness to my spirit. I found myself grappling with how we hold the devastating effects of our collective and personal traumas. As society, how do we intentionally attend to and strengthen mental health? How do we become a society that provides all – young people in particular – with access to means of transcending and transforming trauma?

MaRiky, you were vocal about the reality of depression and mental health in the creative industry. You never missed the opportunity to express your views on the duty each of us has to care for others. How do we build on this, and centre caring and mental health in the fabric of society?

26 March 2022

Dear MaRiky,

The trek today, Saturday, was truly challenging. At 7.30am we started out from Paradise Lounge and Restaurant in Deboche. I suspect that yesterday, 'mountain brain' had already set in with me, because my post has inexplicable references to our trekking team being in Lobuche instead of Deboche (3 400m).

Today we headed for Dingboche, at an altitude of 4 400m.

It seems my body can only promise to carry me if I maintain a pattern of extremely slow, measured movements and breathe intentionally. I comply, and for three and a half hours before lunch, I keep a snail's pace through steep inclines and rocky terrain.

Another three and a half hours of incredibly challenging, slow walking eventually gets me to our tea house. Against the recommendation of our sterling team leader – who advised us to lie down in our sleeping bags and rest for two hours before supper – most of our team stayed huddled around a wood fire/imbawula in the centre of the dining room until supper time. In the cold of this afternoon, we just could not imagine slipping ourselves into our sleeping bags, getting warm and cosy there and thereafter stepping out into the freezing cold in order to have supper. It was too much to contemplate.

For most of today's trek, we walked in silence, giving full attention to the effort of placing one foot in front of the other. In this solitude, the contemplation of yesterday's reflections on mental health continued and delved into the question of healing.

I reflected on an experience where I had called someone out on views that seemed based on racial privilege. I asked her to pause and consider how the views she was sharing negated and erased the lived experience of racism in South Africa. I also reflected on the physical pain I felt in my body at what I took as the violence of racism.

I wondered why this particular incident – which, in all honesty, was not unique and unheard of – had triggered me in such a direct and painful way. I wondered whether the embodied pain was a reflection of the heavy burden that racism and its impacts continue to be. I wondered how the collective South African trauma of racism is actually felt, if the relatively contained experience

I was reflecting on had caused me so much pain and anguish.

I wondered what it would look like for the trauma of racism to be comprehensively surfaced, acknowledged and apologised for, and if effective reparations were to be made. I wondered how and when the people of South Africa might begin to address the lasting effects of the trauma of the apartheid system. In other words, how do we sincerely deal with what was done to us and the manifestations of those misdeeds? I wondered what a South Africa would look like in which all persons, cultures and legacies fully belong, devoid of notions of supremacy and privilege.

Based on all these questions, MaRiky, I need to explore how my personal healing could possibly begin. Even as I highlight personal healing, I am fully aware that race and racism are not personal phenomena. And yet they are so personal in their effects.

Therefore, recognising that the trauma of racism continues to have authority over my body, mind and soul, I wonder whether my healing from this trauma might not start from me claiming my true identity as a divine spiritual being beyond all forms of trauma – personal and collective wounding – towards my transformation as a healing presence in the world. A healing presence to myself and to the community in all its constructions.

This is something I must continue to explore, my love.

Mama

27 March 2022

Dear MaRiky,

It's Sunday today, and we are on our 'active rest day'. This means we could sleep in and only needed to be ready for breakfast at 8am. This is a great reprieve from what has become a routine of starting our daily trek at 7.30am. This late start pleased Aunt Xoli and me tremendously.

We chose to take a two-hour walk to reach 4 600m, before returning to the Peak38 Lodge and Restaurant at 4 400m in time for lunch.

Everything at this altitude is challenging. It starts with simple things like putting on our clothes for the day. The process takes twice the normal time. We are sluggish in so many ways.

The getting dressed part reminds me of a fond childhood memory that my mother – your MaGoegs – had about growing up eMzimvubu, Eastern Cape, spending precious time with MaKhulu, her grandmother.

As the youngest child in her family, MaGoegs had the primary responsibility of caring for MaKhulu. From the age of five, these duties included bringing the first cup of tea exandeni likaMaKhulu (MaKhulu's hut). MaKhulu woke up at 4am sharp every day, without fail.

MaGoegs knew not to start walking with the tea before 8am, because it took MaKhulu four hours to finish her morning dressing up. When MaGoegs knocked on MaKhulu's door, MaKhulu would be tying her last apron string, and ready for her tea. Of course, MaGoegs would have shaken the cup enough to ensure a fair amount of tea had splashed into the saucer.

The two would then gleefully start the day together – MaGoegs sipping tea from the saucer that MaKhulu offered her and Makhulu seated on her chair, sipping from her teacup. I am so happy that you, too, had the blessing of experiencing and being shaped by the special love of your grandmothers. I remember how your friends at Varsity College used to joke about how MaGoegs was your regular ride home from college. It was even a greater joke when your schedule would change, and they would ask if you needed to call your grandma to collect you according to the changed time schedule. For you, MaGoegs being your ride was always special. You loved it!

Your passing was hard for your paternal grandmother, Koko Meims. At the age of ninety-four, Koko Meims made the trip from Polokwane to Johannesburg and was present at the daily prayers and ceremonies held in your honour and for your send-off. She holds very dear the fact that you showed your love and connection to her in your lifetime. She speaks with fondness about the special moments when you would bring the family to visit her at her home in Mankweng, Polokwane and just spend time with her.

Her face always brightens up when she gestures how, on each visit, before you set off to return home, you would take her hand and open up your bulging fist to tickle her heart with a gift of cash. You did well, MaRiky. You honoured your elders while you walked on this end of life. We promise to bear this lasting legacy in reverence.

From this point onwards, cyber connection is quite a challenge, but I have so far been able to keep a sufficiently charged phone, and to play some of your music – particularly when the going gets really rough. Today one of my favourites from the *Family Values* album, 'Bambelela', shored me up through the shuffles and filled me with untold joy. I cherish the knowledge that everywhere, every moment, you are present with me.

    Lots of love,
    Mama

28 March 2022

Dear MaRiky,

Today is Monday, Day 6 of our trek. Our plan was to trek from Dingboche to Laboche in six hours, with an early lunch stop at Thukla. However, this was not to be, as our walk was significantly slower than planned and it took us five hours to reach Thukla. The call was made for us to delay our leg to Lobuche until tomorrow, and we are spending the night in Thukla.

    At this point my concentrated focus is on what thoughts I hold about being here, as I witness our challenges with the altitude. I am drawn to dwelling on the joy, beauty and privilege of being here. I allow my thoughts to rest in the awareness that the experience and my reasons for being on this expedition are far greater than the discomforts borne by the body.

    Accompanying this view is a commitment to give the utmost attention to what is actually happening in the body at all times, and to respond as responsibly as possible.

The excitement continues to build as we approach Base Camp. I am going to conserve energy right now and allow myself to fall asleep.

Love,
Mama

29 March 2022

Dear MaRiky,

Today is Tuesday, Day 7 of our trek. We are moving from Thukla to Laboche. The estimated time for this walk is three hours, but our team does not expect to make it in less than six.

Taking good care of ourselves remains our primary intent, and this is reflected in our walking pace. The images tell the story most poignantly.

Our lodge at Labuche is comfortable and a welcoming space to attend to tired bodies. We lost some days with the cancellation of our planned flight from Johannesburg and the day's delay in reaching Laboche. So our fantastic leader Jeannette will confirm our plan for reaching Base Camp based on her real-time assessment of our circumstances.

Even with this uncertainty around when we will reach Base Camp, the excitement of getting there is palpable. Right now, I have no words for this. I'm playing Aretha Franklin's 'I'm in love', which may say a bit about this excitement...

Love,
Mama

2 April 2022

Dear MaRiky,

Today, Day 11 of the trek, I again wake to the luxurious warmth of an electric blanket and my Nalgene hot-water bottle at Khumbu Lodge, Namche. After several days without the ability to charge phones or send messages, there is a tremendous amount I could say. But only a few words are necessary to convey its essence.

    We finally reached Mount Everest Base Camp on Day 10 of our trek. Aunt Xoli and I were exhilarated! I was caught up in the realisation that I was standing 5 364m above sea level, at this place I had hoped to get to since 2019, before the COVID-19 pandemic intervened. The concrete immediacy of each moment's walking, challenges and lessons had the effect of disaggregating the trek quite significantly. However, arriving at Base Camp brought everything back into focus. In this expansive state, MaRiky, I laid out something of a memorial for you at the Base Camp rock.

    Your beloved wife Bianca, and your children Jordan and Maik, had sent me off with a few memorabilia. Singing the Methodist Xhosa Hymn 259, 'Ndinik'amehlo Ndikhangele', I laid out a 'Riky Rick… We Multiply' T-shirt on the rock. Above it was a chain containing three items. There was a medallion of St Michael – the archangel who helps us in our hour of death – as a symbolic representation of Bianca and the kids' prayers. A St Christopher medallion represented my travel prayers for all of us. Finally, a medallion with a 'MaRiky' engraving hung on that chain, a beautiful product of the talented, young jewellers at the tattoo joint that your friends recently opened in Braam Square. I laid it as your family's commitment to carrying forward your legacy of supporting and caring for young people.

At Base Camp, everything came together in that amazing 'contraction-and-expansion' pattern of the universe, MaRiky. All I could do at this point was to keep bowing in gratitude, joy, peace and hope. I could never find the words to clearly set out the depth of awakening I experienced coming to Base Camp and communicating with you through ritual.

Thank you for helping me to come to such knowing and feeling, MaRiky.

Thank you so much for enabling so many to connect with your family, your loved ones and I, and to hold us up in immense love and generous support as we continue to grieve your departure from this realm of life, together.

I love you MaRiky.

We can never forget you.

Mama

In the beginning

My parents, Florida Ntombizanele Zondo (neé Mayeza) and William 'Bill' Zondo, named me Louisa Barbara Zondo. I am the last of three sisters. Tandi Faith Zondo is five years my senior and Jacqueline 'Jackie' Marie Zondo is eighteen months older than I am. I was born in KwaMashu, an African township some 12km north-west of the central business district of the city of Durban. The South African system of apartheid classified people into the racial groups of African, coloured, Indian and white. On the basis of this classification, racial segregation and the erasure of the humanity of people who were not classified as white people was entrenched in all aspects of South African life, including spatial planning.

In urban settings those classified white lived in sprawling suburbs located in pristine areas of the country, while people who were classified as black (African, coloured and Indian) lived in densely populated townships featuring rows of uniform structures with a maximum of four rooms for housing and a smattering of amenities. Indian townships were more resourced than the ones designated coloured, and African townships were at the bottom of the rung.

KwaMashu was built in 1957, and large numbers of people who had been forcibly and brutally removed from urban communities such as Cato Manor, where different people of varying racial categorisations lived together, were moved to the township. It was organised into distinct sections, and A Section was a massive men's hostel. Its purpose was to house the African men who had been compelled to join the wage labour force in the urban areas. Mass forced removals, land dispossessions, and the imposition of a poll tax on African people had destroyed the sustainability and self-sufficiency of people's lives and livelihoods in rural, urban and peri-urban areas. Men, in the first instance, were compelled to migrate in large numbers to urban areas to seek jobs and lived in hostels such as KwaMashu's A Section.

PARADOXICALLY, WHILE THE apartheid system needed a good supply of manual labour, it had a fear of an influx of people who were not classified white. A raft of draconian apartheid laws (the Pass Laws) was enacted and brutally enforced. These laws ensured the imprisonment of masses of African people above the age of sixteen for failing to produce proof of their identification and valid permits to be in an urban area when called upon to do so.

Pass Laws dehumanised and criminalised African people in South Africa. They controlled people's movement while keeping people segregated and allocating labour in a manner that institutionalised the dream of one of the principal architects of apartheid, Hendrik F Verwoerd (Minister of Native Affairs, 1940-1948 and Prime Minister, 1948-1966). His dream was that apartheid would confine African people to being 'hewers of wood and drawers of water'.

The Natives Land Act, Act No 27 of 1913, was a significant landmark as it framed into legislation an oppressive, violent system of land dispossession which had started under earlier colonial regimes. It resulted in land ownership by Africans (who constituted more than 80% of the South African population) being restricted to 13% of the country's land, leaving more than

70% of land in the hands of white people who made up less than 8% of the population.

KwaMashu was named after a sugarcane farm owner Sir Marshall Campbell, who reportedly donated the land on which it is built. In Zulu it means 'at the place of Marshall'. Up until the late 1970s, when the coloured township Newlands East was built alongside, KwaMashu had only one entrance on Ntombela Road, starting at E Section and meandering through the township to end at B Section.

The Township Administration Office building and the KwaMashu Police Station prominently marked the entrance. Access into and out of KwaMashu was controlled by the highly visible presence and actions of the South African Police and the lower-ranking and often more brutal township municipal police (derisively referred to as the Black Jacks). In the 1980s, as the Zulu Police gained jurisdiction, they engaged in higher levels of brutality. The place was hard to take in – aesthetically and in many other ways. Crime, violence and gangsterism became the focal point of KwaMashu caricature and anecdotes, earning it names such as Kwamfaz'ushay'indoda (the place where the woman beats up the man) or Esinqawunqawini (the place where dog eats dog).

KWAMASHU WAS ALWAYS A contender for South Africa's murder capital, unequivocally snatching that title in 2009 when it recorded 300 murders. Comparative studies of murder rates in KwaMashu and another Durban township Umlazi confirm that the rate of serious offences such as murder and attempted murder is higher in KwaMashu which has a population just over half that of Umlazi. The findings reported in a 1987 study, 'The Extent and Nature of Crime in Umlazi and KwaMashu' by LE Glanz and HG Strydom, were that the murder and attempted murder rate in KwaMashu was seven times the South African rate.

My parents secured a house at F Section, house number F264 KwaMashu soon after my eldest sister Tandi was born in 1959. Parents destined to raise their children amidst the squalid conditions of KwaMashu and the plethora of other challenges associated with apartheid had to make certain choices to protect their children and increase their prospects for better lives. My parents' choices were clear. They were intent on ensuring our compliance with extremely stringent rules.

These rules included: remaining confined to the home perimeter at all times with no unsupervised visits to neighbours or to play with other children on the streets or anywhere else; only to play with children of relatives and family friends visiting our home in the company of their parents; only English was to be spoken at home; to always eat at the table even at snack times (Milo or cold milk and buttered bread); and to set the table properly for meals, follow table etiquette and specifically master the elegant use of a fork and knife at an early age.

We had no option but to attend primary school in the township, but our school life was also centred on non-mainstream home rules such as healthy sandwiches for lunch and no lunch money at all; no stop-overs or delays at schools after classes were dismissed; no involvement in any fighting whatsoever; wear clean socks and shoes every day and keep them on all the time while at school; and our behaviour at school was to be flawless. We were required to maintain discipline and be diligent in our learning.

We could not escape being severely teased by other children for our lifestyle. We were called Abelungu abamnyama (black whites). Not only did this pain us deeply, I also felt self-conscious for being different. I wished I had been allowed to be with, and be like, other children. At an early age, I developed an aversion to anything that tended to make me stand out from the rest. I knew of no other family that had this English language rule.

When I was in my late teens, my mother explained to my sisters and me that those rules were an attempt to do the best they could to raise us up and prepare us for better prospects. Because of the apartheid system's intentions and effects of subverting the humanity of black people and rendering us devoid of possibilities, capabilities and imagination, they wanted us to be exposed to the ways of life of white people, so that we would not feel inferior to them and unfamiliar with their ways.

My mother understood and empathised with us, when we told her that our experience of following the rules was quite different from what they had intended. My English at high school was not by any measure better than the English spoken by my friends who had not been subjected to a language rule in their homes. Our subtle resistance manifested in us speaking English in a tone that was very strongly Zulu. Even today, I lack confidence when I speak English in settings where the participants are in the main first-language English speakers. I become uncomfortable at the prospect of pronouncing words in ways that would affect what I intend to communicate.

Participating in the Moot Court trial programme in 1986 during my final year of an LLB degree at Howard College, University of KwaZulu-Natal, suggested that I had good reason to be conscious of my pronunciation and enunciation. I made it to the Moot Court finals with a partner and an article in the college's law magazine that reviewed its hilarious and peculiar moments reported my reference to raising 'the human cry' when I had spoken of raising 'the hue and cry'. After sharing laughs with friends about the article, I allowed myself disappointment at being misheard, although I retained the honour of being in one of the top four Moot Court trialists in 1986.

My father was born on 2 October 1930 in Bulwer, a small town in the breathtakingly beautiful region of the Midlands in the KwaZulu-Natal province. The Amahwaqa Mountain (the misty one), which is highly acclaimed for paragliding, forms its backdrop. My father was raised in a home in the Nkelabantwana village. His family was not wealthy and was among the early adopters of Christianity in the area. The community of Christians came to be called Emakholweni (the place of believers), distinguished from those who remained steeped in their traditional ways of life.

My father had two older brothers, Maudy and Windam, and two sisters, Bettina and Bellecia. He was the youngest. As an adult, I learnt that my father had a third brother who had not embraced Christianity. I am told by a cousin who remained in Nkelabantwana that he was a healer and therefore felt stifled amongst the staunch

Christians. One day he took his inyanga's (healer's) bag, left home in the direction of Kokstad and was never heard from again.

A devout Christian from an early age, my father was taken into the home of the head minister of the Pholela mission as a teenager and was raised as part of his family, while he attended high school at Pholela Institution. He maintained some contact with his own family, the Zondos. I learnt from my mother that after completing matric he and the minister's son travelled together from Bulwer to Durban to apply for jobs. They found an opening in the public administration that appealed to them. Both applied for the job and were interviewed. My father was offered the position, and that was the last contact he had with the minister's son and the rest of the family. My mother was unable to shed any light on the mysteries of this relationship, she had only superficial information about my father's life in Pholela. I never asked any questions about my father's childhood when he was alive, and the scant knowledge I have about his upbringing is one of the most powerful mysteries of my life.

Until 2013 I had never spent time in Bulwer. While I was at high school our family travelled there for Aunt Bellecia's funeral but my father made it a day trip, driving us back to Durban after the graveside service. I never met the white family that so intimately overlaps with my own.

This rather strange experience is an example of how the tyranny of apartheid cut families off from each other, destroyed real human relationships and caused humans to develop quite destructive, fear-based protection mechanisms while attempting to create better lives for their loved ones. It is the story of my life.

From early childhood my life was shaped by many, many rules. Following them became akin to a matter of life and death and the art of asking curious questions became significantly numbed. Skirting over things and not probing beneath the surface became part of my make-up. I needed to keep my authority figures happy by remaining within the bounds of the systems they set. I could not break any of my parents' house rules. When I think about myself as a child I see young Louisa standing behind the perimeter fence at home, watching the neighbourhood children playing.

My mother was born on 30 October 1930 according to her national identity document, but she was born a year earlier in 1929. She was delivered into the Mayeza family in the Transkei in an area called Ekutsheni, overlooking the Mzimvubu River. Her home was surrounded by tall trees. As a child, I was filled with emotion when I would see from afar as we drove towards Mount Frere that cluster of tall trees and the white ruins that were the remains of my mother's home. I heard many times from my mother how my grandfather John Mayeza and his wife uMaKhumalo had been quite the entrepreneurs, starting and successfully operating a money-lending business and becoming prominent personalities in the Mount Frere area and beyond. My mother told of white men coming to her home to borrow money from her father.

My grandmother had given birth to eleven children and four had died in infancy. My mother was the last-born and battled a severe bronchial ailment which was never diagnosed but was persistently treated with amafutha ezinja zolwandle (cod liver oil) until she overcame it in her teenage years. Her stories about my grandmother conjured up images of an ever-active, busy and diligent person who managed the physical infrastructure of a large homestead as well as its cropping and animal-husbandry operations, while her husband saw to the money-lending business. I am proud that I inherited from my grandmother a right leg that juts out, as if I have one knock knee. My mother told me that, because my grandmother had quite a large body, the jutting out of her right leg was particularly prominent, while it is possible to miss mine if one is not paying much attention to my legs. My mother's brothers were all provided with a good education, qualifying as teachers and agricultural inspectors. However, alcoholism got the better of all of them and none could keep a job. After their parents' deaths they literally ran the family business into the ground, leaving the ruins that we saw from afar while driving into Mount Frere.

THE MZIMVUBU AREA IS INHABITED by amaBhaca and my mother thoroughly enjoys some of their ways such as eating meat cooked extremely rare, a practice called ukufukuta. She enjoyed tending to the family's herd of animals even though she suffered bullying from her brothers because she was a girl and the youngest of her mother's children. She was the same age as her nephew Mzamo, who was raised as a sibling after his mother died shortly after childbirth, leaving him and his sister Thandeka. My mother's pained experience was losing a place of affection when everyone in the family poured their sympathy and love into the two young ones who had lost their mother.

My mother's life story is one of sheer determination not to have her spirit crushed. Even with the bullying and constantly being pitted against Mzamo in fights orchestrated by her brothers for their entertainment – and always ending in tears when Mzamo defeated her – she never stopped going into the veld to tend to the livestock with the males. Her ability to count meticulously stood her in good stead and she learnt everything about livestock. My mom's ultimate pride when we slaughtered a sheep at my home (to welcome each grandchild) was that by using her fist, she could skin the whole animal neatly without leaving a piece of flesh on the skin. She was also proud of her skills in cleaning the intestines. She would tie a knot at one end and move all the material in the intestines towards that end, and then seal the sac and run tap water down the length before chopping it up in preparation for the most delicious tripe dish.

My mother completed her Junior Certificate at Shawbury Mission in the Eastern Cape and studied for a teacher's diploma. She taught in Mount Frere for a while and later transferred to Tabankulu in a village called Mnceba where she lived with SoMncane, the younger of her two older sisters. Her brother-in-law Mr Gumpe was principal at Mnceba Secondary School, and my mother enjoyed her time at this school. She rode her white horse, Bob, to school. She loved him dearly and described him as a true beauty with a gait to match. Bob had to be put down after he balked and fell, breaking a few bones.

THE OTHER WOMEN IN MY mother's home also received some education. Her sisters SoPhakathi and SoMncane completed domestic science courses after their primary education. My mother wanted to become a professional and dreamt of teaching. However, she was not allowed to enrol for the teacher's diploma immediately after school because her brothers persuaded their father, who was educated up to Standard Five, that tertiary education for a woman was fruitless and inspired scandalous conduct. SoMncane's husband came to her rescue and convinced her father that if she came to live with them in Tabankulu, she would complete her teacher training without going astray. Her father conceded.

An unexpected experience with a mail-order face cream changed my mother's life and shaped the destiny of generations of our family. She saw an advertisement and purchased it via mail order. After she used the cream, her entire face broke out into a septic wound. She sought treatment, but it soon became apparent that the local doctors were unable to help. It was eventually decided that she would have to travel to Durban for treatment at McCord Hospital. She spent several months in hospital and fortunately recovered. However, she was infected by the nursing bug and realised that she could not continue teaching.

Her family was not happy at all with this prospect. She was the youngest and a woman, so again her brothers considered it their duty to shape the decisions her parents took about her life choices. Her brother advised that going off to the big city to enrol as a nurse would ruin her. But my mother was determined. She packed up and went off for nursing training in Durban. She had the blessings of her sisters and SoMncane's husband Mr Gumpe, and that gave significant meaning to her life.

A devout young Methodist, she joined the Wesley Guild and actively participated in its activities aimed at keeping young people within the church fold. She particularly loved ballroom dancing and attending socials. The ballroom dancing, doing the foxtrot and waltzing at City Hall, would remain among her life's glory days.

When asked about the story of her courtship with my father, her face would light up. They met at the Wesley Guild on the ballroom-dance scene. She considered him a dignified young man, tall and rather self-aware. He showed an interest in her, but she was terrified of any kind of romance. Her fears stemmed from seeing the lives of too many young nurses crumble from depressing betrayals, unplanned pregnancies or death from illegal abortions. She was a rural girl, quite happy with her new nursing career and the fun to be found at the Guild socials.

She slowly came to realise that this young man was probably not like most of the other, swift-moving young suitors. He remained a constant presence even though they were never ballroom dance partners. He was certainly part of the scene but his forte was in lay preaching, especially articulating arguments during debates in a way that allowed English to flow through the nose. Spoken English was a feature of my father's character and his culture, because of his upbringing. It took some time, but something about my father's proper manner appealed to my mother and they were married on 16 December 1958.

THE WEDDING TOOK PLACE AT the school hall in Mnceba, and SoMncane and Mr Gumpe provided the bridal home. SoMncane also sewed my mother's beautiful wedding gown.

Then too, as is the case now, 16 December was a public holiday. For people of the time, some prestige was attached to a couple being able to declare that they were truly married and assert that they 'closed the school' for the wedding. Because my parents had their wedding on a public holiday, they never interrupted the schooling. No community fanfare was occasioned by their wedding. This notwithstanding, the marriage proved a success. With meticulous precision, my eldest sister Tandi was born on 28 September 1959. Almost two years later on 16 August 1962 my second sister Jackie was born, and I joined the family eighteen months after Jackie, on 5 February 1964.

Soon after Tandi was born, my parents moved into their four-roomed house at F264, KwaMashu. My father worked for the administration, starting off as a clerk in the black administration offices. He later enrolled to study for a degree in social work and graduated from the University of Natal. Thereafter, he worked as a social worker at child welfare.

After my mother completed her training at McCord Hospital, she started working at King Edward Hospital before moving to the Kwamashu polyclinic. With their meagre salaries, my parents managed their family resourcefully. My mother augmented her nurse's salary with money she earned from dressmaking. She bought underwear in bulk and beautified it by adding lace trims. At the polyclinic, all types of underwear sold like hot cakes. My duty from the age of four was to massage my mother's legs by squeezing them with my legs. She used to joke about how she imagined me getting bendy legs from the seriously hard squeezing I would have to do to relax her legs after she had toiled for hours at the foot-pedal Singer sewing machine.

DESPITE THEIR FINANCIAL CHALLENGES, when I was growing up my parents always had a car. After I was born, I came home in a brand-new 1964 Morris Minor. Every day my father prepared himself for the working day by putting on a freshly ironed clean shirt and a neatly pressed suit. He did not own many such garments at first, but there was routine that ensured that he always had a crisp, fresh shirt for work and his suit was always professionally pressed, with no shine from burnt fibres. My family would have supper together at the dinner table. The table would be properly set with place mats, side plates, cutlery and serviettes. On Saturdays my father did our weekly shopping at the market, and every week I watched with some fascination as my mother gave him the budgeted amount for fruit, vegetables and groceries. He would thank her and drive off to the market. My mother was an entrepreneur by nature and her ladies' underwear range expanded to beautiful petticoats. She would take these stylish, quality garments to work and sell them to colleagues and patients. People would also purchase them as gifts. Her repertoire grew to everything from lumber jackets to dresses, in particular beautiful wrap-around dresses.

In 1984 the organisers of a local debutantes' ball approached my mother with a request to design and sew dresses for all the entrants. She created something like twenty white ballgowns, and all the young women looked smashing in their gorgeous, glamorous floor-length dresses. The fundraising ball was a success. It required incredible dedication to do the dressmaking work on top of her full-time nursing responsibilities. It made a significant contribution to our household finances and allowed my parents to build the kind of life they believed was best for their family. The car, neat home, dresses and suits reflected their vision for their family. Their aspiration to encounter white culture head-on and not be intimidated had particular significance for them, even if they had to work many times harder to achieve just an approximation of it. My mother didn't mind too much what she wore, but she always looked great because she was an immaculate dressmaker. She was skilled at styling her hair and blessed with a beautiful, dimpled face with flawless skin.

The furniture in our house was basic but sturdy. We never had the high-value pieces that were revered in township homes, brands such as GommaGomma or Grafton Everest lounge suites, room dividers or expensive music systems. Our dining room had a faithful brown couch that opened into a reliable sleeper couch for occasional visitors. We had a dining table, sideboard, a bookcase with two stained-glass doors and an old-style Blaupunkt AM/FM radio-record player console. It stood on four legs and had thick, brown embroidery over its speakers. In the kitchen, we had a basic table with four chairs, a paraffin fridge and a black coal stove, later upgraded to a more deluxe shiny yellow one.

We children slept in one room. We had two single beds; two girls would sleep in one bed and the third would share with the person who lived with us, helping with domestic work and caring for us. Later when we moved to B Section and had more space in the house, a bunk bed was added to our room. This meant we only shared beds when we had guests sleeping over. A small, free-standing wardrobe completed the furnishings in our room. Our parents' bedroom had twin beds pulled together, two wardrobes and a dressing table with an oval mirror.

My father was a Western classical music enthusiast, so I

grew up hearing Handel, Mozart, Strauss, Bach and other great composers in the house and in the car. When my father took us to a Durban Philharmonic Orchestra performance of Handel's Messiah at the City Hall, I was surprised at the enormity of the thrill I got from watching the orchestra. Until I was about eleven years old, classical music was my major exposure to culture. While we had a radio, it was not something we children used. I picked up the music of the time from sounds in the neighbourhood and learnt a few of the popular dance moves of the era. Popular songs in the early 1970s such as 'Guava Jelly' by Johnny Nash and Al Green's 'Love and Happiness' pleased my heart and so did local love songs from artists like Babsy Mlangeni, and Mahlathini & The Mahotella Queens.

We were governed by our parents' rules. I would come home from school and make myself a glass of Milo with milk and a bread-and-butter sandwich. These would be consumed seated at the kitchen table, with the sandwich on a side plate and the Milo in a plastic cup. Unlike today, a meal was never something to be rushed, eaten while standing or on the go while doing something else.

In those days, milk was delivered to the front door. Two or three times a week, we would find two glass bottles of cold milk on the doorstep, fresh with condensation and sealed with a foil cap. There were also rules for bringing in the milk. It was a luxury and therefore treated with extreme care. You never shook the bottle after picking it up. You held it steady to preserve the cream at the top for my father's morning coffee.

Dinner would be a basic meal, perhaps also in the English tradition. There would be soup served with bread, a main course with at least two vegetables, a starch and meat, followed by dessert. It would be cooked in different ways, which might still deliver the odd surprise. Sometimes I would tuck into my stew, chewing on what I expected to be a potato, only to discover it was a turnip – a far less inviting prospect. My mother cooked regularly, but it was my father who had ideas about how things should be prepared. Even though theirs was a traditional patriarchal arrangement, my mother was not overshadowed by my father. She was filled with energy and was the engine that helped drive our family's trajectory through life in KwaMashu.

My parents decided to improve their financial position by establishing a formal business. At the time local shops were viable businesses and shop owners were counted among the rich in the township. Being educated and a professional brought the necessary esteem and respect in the community but their meagre salaries did not go far enough towards providing for the family's financial needs. When my parents ran their shop full time, it was my mother's consistent focus that kept it thriving. My father continued his board engagements at Child Welfare and was involved in church structures. He was also involved in the establishment and the affairs of the provincial black business chamber, Inyanda, and the National Federation of Chambers of Commerce, Nafcoc. He frequently travelled overseas as a tourist and to attend Christian conferences.

Every time he left on a trip, my mother would be flushed with excitement as she challenged herself to improve the business while he was away. She would arrange promotions to stimulate more traffic into the shop. I was always pleased when my father was away because it meant I slept with my mother in her bed.

I loved my mother's soothing energy. Even as she worked hard, she did it with joy and ease. A truly committed and focused person, she always sought to reach new goals and to achieve higher standards.

THE GIRL STANDING IN OUR YARD, peering over the fence at the neighbourhood kids playing and feeling so imprisoned by the rules – that's still me. I remember feeling a deep, palpable sadness.

I started school aged five. My first school was Dumani Lower Primary School (LP5) in G Section in KwaMashu. I remember holding the hem of my school dress and undoing it, tearing it loose with the sheer anxiety of my feelings. Usually, my dress would be a bit too short because I was meant to wear it for a long time and my mother let down part of the huge hem as I grew taller. My habit always got me into trouble. I'm not sure whether subconsciously I wanted dresses of a more respectable length, or dresses that that had been worn for fewer years. The trouble caused by letting out the hem made me even more anxious, yet I could not stop. Looking back, I see that this pattern of behaviour accompanied me throughout my life.

I also felt anxious and sad when my sisters got into trouble; they broke the rules more than I did. We had a cousin who sometimes lived with us, Uncle Windam's daughter Dudu. She was petite and frail and may have been affected by allergies because her eyes were dark around the edges, and she seemed to struggle with her sight. Dudu was five years older than me – the same age as my eldest sister. I wanted to love and protect her, put her inside my skin and keep her safe, even though I was younger. Dudu was never going to cope with all the rules, she did not come from such an environment, and she was vibrant. She was free to speak isiZulu and play in the streets. But despite the compelling drive to be good, I was constantly in trouble. Dudu would also get into trouble for everything from going out of the yard to breaking the language rule or deviating from dinner table etiquette.

After my second year of primary school, in January 1971, we left F section as my parents wanted to live in B Section to be closer to their shop. My mother later told me that after a few months of working at the shop and returning home at about 9pm, they had detected that something had changed with us. They did not know what it was, but they knew that they needed to urgently bring us closer to them.

The decision to relocate was quite sudden and left us sad. In the four months our parents had been operating the shop, we had turned into three wild cats. The woman who looked after us was new, and she was happy to let us roam the neighbourhood all day. She cooked a staple of mincemeat and rice and never set the table, allowing us to eat in the kitchen and then to run off to play with the neighbours' children. I most enjoyed Dumbezi's home, two doors from ours. The family belonged to the African Zionist church. They wore all-white uniforms with green belts and trimmings. I enjoyed their services because most of the time it was rhythmic singing and movement, and the beat of the drum. I have no recollection of long sermons at these services. Whether I joined the service from outside or inside their house, I was filled with joy.

Around 8.30pm, the woman who looked after us would call us to get back indoors and we would run back home, wipe our feet clean and slip into bed. The shop closed at 8pm, and after 30 minutes to cash up, my parents reached our home around 9pm. We didn't want them to catch us breaking their rules and made sure we returned home promptly when we were called. This taste of freedom was unbelievable. I was excited all the time. I could ask Lolo, the twelve-year-old son of Miss Mathe across from our house, to teach me to walk on my hands in the street. I could ask him to give me a ride on his hand-made scooters – both the upright and the flat one. It did not matter that I never learnt how to keep my balance on his scooters, or to steer the contraptions. The joy was in the ability to connect with children in the neighbourhood. Moving to B Section brought all of this to a screeching halt.

We were told that our parents were swopping our house – which had been slightly improved from a standard township four-roomed house – with one that had no improvements at all. We loved our veranda, which was added by our parents. On hot summer nights my parents would bring the dining table out onto the veranda, and we would eat dinner outdoors. This I unashamedly enjoyed. I really love avocado. We had an avocado tree in the front of the house which had not borne fruit for the first six years of my life. But in 1970 we saw supple heads on the tree and were looking forward to enjoying creamy Durban avocado from our beautiful tree. It pained me that I would have to leave it without ever tasting its fruit. Our house also had a peach and mulberry tree. There was a hedge made of granadilla vines in the back garden and to this day, I cannot bring myself to pay for granadilla.

To reach our outside toilet, we would pass the fowl run in the garden. It housed turkeys from time to time, annoying geese – and once we even had rabbits that stayed too long. With livestock, the idea was to keep them only a short period before they could be slaughtered for the pot. But by the time my mother slaughtered the rabbits, all of us – my father included – had built a relationship with them and were in two minds about eating them.

What distinguished the new house in B Section was that it had electricity. We were pleasantly surprised by the quick renovations that had been done to the very basic house before we moved in. My parents converted the front rooms to a dining room and lounge and added a passage out of the kitchen that led to a bathroom and toilet on one side and a bedroom on the other.

Having electricity and an indoor toilet and bathroom were a great source of pride, especially having a bathtub. Previously bathing had required half-filling an iron bath with boiling water from the stove in the kitchen. This would be carried to the outside toilet and topped up with cold water from the shower. It was the responsibility of my sister Tandi to help me bath at our old house in F Section. She would mix the water to get it just right for me. But I would torture her because occasional drops of cold water from the shower would fall and run down my back, and I would scream at my sister with dismay.

We moved over the weekend and I was to start at my new school – Ethekwini Lower Primary School, LP 18 – on the Monday. Again, I found myself in a child's conundrum, caught between the excitement of the first day of school, wanting to make my parents proud and the fear of getting into trouble. I woke early on that first day, to prepare for school. The indoor bathroom hadn't been built yet and I washed myself with water from the kitchen sink. My sisters were not yet awake, and I was desperate to make sure they were not late for school. My soon to be seven-year-old mind found a solution; the best way to save everybody precious time was to prepare three sets of sandwiches for school lunch. That became a part of our daily routine. For the rest of our school careers, I prepared sandwiches for Jackie and Tandi every day before school. I needed to make people happy and ensure that everything was organised, and that became my habit at home and in life.

Our shop was on my route to school. My mom was always

there. She would arrive early, get things ready and let customers in at 7am. She would remain there into the night, every day, 365 days a year. Before going to school, I would make her a cup of tea. During the first school break, I would sprint out of the gates and run to the shop, which was just behind the school. I ran to relieve my mother, who by then had been behind the till for several hours and needed a bathroom break. When we opened the store I became adept at taking cash from customers and calculating their change, so I could take my mother's place at the till for a few minutes. A perk for filling in for my mom was being given permission to help myself to a bottle of Fanta and a coconut cake before running back to school.

Ethekwini LP 18 was an improvement on my previous school, Dumani, where I spent a nasty two years. When I started at Dumani I could already count to 100 and beyond. I was comfortable with basic arithmetic. So, when Miss began teaching us the names of the numbers from one to five, I was soon frustrated and bored to tears. What saved me was the fact that I was shy. Precocious children were not popular at Dumani LP 5; I would probably have received a quick smack had I asked Miss to teach us all the numbers up to 100 and told her that I had already learned multiplication from my older sisters. I learned to hold my tongue and to do the work that was put in front of me.

Fortunately, the new school was better. Now in Standard One, we started doing comprehension tests. We learned to write cursive, and for the first time I had some exposure to rural life. Given my upbringing, my first experience of rural amaZulu culture came through my isiZulu language lessons. Our comprehension essays were about how to build umuzi (a traditional Zulu hut). IsiZulu was our language of instruction. Only our English lesson was given in English. I was excited to learn about Zulu customs and culture, especially when I was asked to write an essay about the brewing of Zulu beer. This had some resonance for me, because the shop sold ingredients for preparing utshwala besiZulu (Zulu beer).

I began to develop a deeper love for Zulu culture as we began to learn expressive idioms that drew on its traditions and way of life. The idiomatic expression Akusensuku zatshwala means in less than a week and literally translates as less than the days required to fully brew beer. This comes from the concept that seven days are required to brew the beer properly for traditional functions.

In Standard One I also learned idiomatic expressions such as selidumela emansumpeni, which means you are close to the end and refers to the altered sound at a point close to the handles of a calabash. As the vessel fills up the sound reaches a higher pitch, so one says selidumela emansumpeni when a matter is getting close to finality. These expressions were conveyed to us orally. It was only in Standard Four or Five that we received our first Zulu textbooks and could learn more idioms.

My Standard One teacher was Miss Zungu and she taught us everything from scripture to English to isiZulu. In Standard Two, we had the iconic Miss Mtshali. She demanded excellence and kept the exercise books of top students from previous years as a way of motivating her current students.

'You see!' she would say. 'This one never got less than 10 out of 10!' This caused some friction in the neighbourhood.

'Why did you have to be showing off last year?' the younger kids would berate the older ones. 'Now Miss Mtshali expects us to get 10 out of 10.' Recently I met a young man who had also attended LP 18 and who had been in Miss Mtshali's class. He said that she was so encouraging of his efforts that she bought him a present one year. She bought him a toy!

I thrived on this culture of excellence and managed to have my books included in Miss Mtshali's showcase for future years. But on the social front, I hardly had friends. I was too afraid of getting into trouble. At that school, if somebody decided to tell someone else that you had said something unpleasant about them, you would be called to a fight. These were physical fist fights which were called a perro. I believe the term comes from Portuguese, and it was a terrifying prospect for me. I wasn't small for my age, but I was gentle and introverted, which meant I could never be involved in a fight. I was more afraid of the girls than the boys.

I would have happily kept a low profile, but my father did not make this easy. He got it into his mind that Jackie and I were not going to do what the school rules required. We were not going to shave our hair into a chiskop like every other child at the school. We were going to grow out our locks and go to school with plaited hair.

How our eldest sister escaped that innovation I don't know, but we had no option. I was the only one in my class with that hairstyle. After I passed on a message from the teacher saying I must cut my hair, I was ordered to say: 'My father says I must tell you that your duty is to teach and that you should not be concerned about our hair.'

I was at pains to help my teachers realise that I was not an insolent child. I was also terrified of being seen as different by the other girls. That was difficult when I looked so different. I overheard threats in the corridors to pull my braids. I could only imagine the pain of being pulled, so I tried desperately to keep a low profile.

But the children at school would overhear me at the shop saying 'Yes, mummy' in response to my mother calling me, and word soon was out that we spoke English at home. 'You actually are becoming a black white,' I was told. The implication was that we thought we were better than the rest of our community.

The only friend I had in the early years at LP 18 was Bathabile Mahaye, another relatively quiet child. Her father was friends with mine. Like me she had eczema, although hers was in more visible places than mine. We shared lunch. She thought my sandwiches were heavenly and in return gave me five cents every day. Bathabile trained as a social worker. Then, in her fifties, she transitioned to law and is now an attorney in Cape Town.

At primary school I was seldom found playing on the playground. At least one school break every day, I would relieve my mother at the shop. Our lives changed because of the shop. Previously, on Sundays we would go to church and for a drive after lunch. At Christmas we would drive into town to see the lights and do some window shopping. But shop life meant our church routine fell away. Our father introduced a new way of looking at our relationship with God. He had been a lay preacher in the

Methodist Church and taught us that, 'God expects you to be in prayer and in connection with him at all times. This idea that you need to go to church on Sunday in order to be in connection with him is completely misplaced.' Our 6pm prayers at home ended because the shop closed at 8pm.

My dad became embroiled in the black business movement with leaders including Dr Sam Motsoenyane and Dr Richard Maponya. They were examining how black business could consolidate power and become a phenomenal force for positive change. One of their first initiatives was the Black Chain – a fully black-owned business centre in Soweto. In Natal the business chamber was called the Inyanda Chamber of Commerce, and it was part of the National African Federated Chambers of Commerce and Industry. Although it was a business chamber, it had a very clear political role. It emerged from the reality that we are black, maligned, discriminated against and had to find ways to bring our capacities together to reach our full potential. That was my father's motivation.

After the Black Chain was established we were excited about the enormous mall in the township, evidence of the work being done. It was the first state-of-the-art mall built by black people, an enormous source of pride. In this spirit of growth, we expanded our operations. Our shop started as a small store, like many of the time. People would enter, go to the counter, and ask for what they wanted to buy. Some items were displayed on shelves behind the counter and bulk goods were kept at the storeroom at the back. A popular purchase that had to be brought from the back would be the ingredients for beer. That was called i-set and consisted of two loaves of brown bread, sorghum meal, maize meal, brown sugar and yeast – all in the right proportions.

In the original configuration of the shop, someone might request two sets. The staff would head into the back to prepare the package. The customer would wait for their order to be prepared. Amidst all this activity my mother would be the only person handling the cash. At times, the rush of people returning from work and demanding to be served would be a crowd – of mainly men – filling the space from the counter to the back of the room. Behind the counter there was just enough space for the staff to hand over purchases and take the cash to my mother so she could make change. Sis Mamsy, one of my mother's lifelong friends and also a former teacher, worked in the shop and was a huge support to my mother.

Inspired by the idea of black business excellence, my parents expanded the shop into a supermarket. It had two sections. One had the original counter-service system, while the new section featured aisles with products on display for customers to select and place in their shopping baskets. A trellis divider separated the shopping space from the counter-service area and the cashier. Shoppers would enter and choose a shopping route, then queue to pay the cashier. The new shop was called Zan-Will Supermarket after the names of my parents, Zanele and William.

The new supermarket represented a fundamental break with the past. Some people were traumatised by it and would not enter the supermarket. Among them was Mr Shange who lived in the hostel. He wore his pierced ears hanging nice and loose and would enter the shop after work, his khaki uniform still neat, with crisply ironed seams. He was orderly in the extreme, plainly someone who had stayed in a job for many years, had huge respect for rules and expected everybody else to behave similarly. He was close to the caricature of gqayinyanga, the immovable Zulu security guard. This kind of person would not open a gate for anybody. Once they had been instructed not to let anyone pass, there would be no entrance whatsoever – even for the boss.

It seemed he had never learned English, but he spoke it regardless. He would step inside the entrance of the shop but go no further. He would wait to be served.

My father honoured Mr Shange and would greet him politely. 'Good afternoon, Mr Shange, how are you?'

'Very good.'

'What can I do for you, Mr Shange?'

'One sheleni shugela. One sheleni fulawa. Two katoni amasi!'

All my parents' employees knew they had to listen carefully

and rush around to serve him.

The new system brought another aspect to our jobs. It was called 'help customers' but it was a form of security. A staff member had to have eyes on every aisle at all times. When a customer entered we would be careful not to bombard them, but we made it clear that we were there. Some people were annoyed by our constant vigilance, so we would move to the back and keep an eye on things from there to limit how much was stolen by customers.

The shop was where I first got a sense of different ways in which people lived. Certain families would come to the shop at breakfast time, lunch time and supper time. It was obvious that they were buying for the next meal only – whether it was two eggs, a tomato and an onion; half a nip of oil; mielie rice; half a bottle of paraffin. Customers who had a bit more to work with would buy a gallon of paraffin at a time, enough to last a week or a month. Mainly, people were buying for the moment, unlike my father who shopped weekly for his family.

I was tasked with handling the cash and some adult customers struggled to trust that a little one like myself would give them the right change. But my parents trusted me. When people disputed their change, they would always defend me. To earn that trust, I had to concentrate furiously. Accuracy was built into our system. All transactions were announced aloud to the entire store. 'You gave me fifty cents, right? The Amasi is twenty-nine cents. Twenty-nine. Thirty. Forty. Fifty!'

The shop was in the family until I went to university. My entire childhood was spent there. The growth and eventual end of the business follows the same arc of our journey as a family. My father had a vision to develop the business. The first step was the supermarket, where I worked every day of my life while I was at LP 18. My higher primary school was in C Section, KwaMashu, which was further away. I would arrive at 3pm, change out of my school uniform, have my lunch, which was always left-over supper from the previous evening, and work in the shop until 6pm. For high school I was sent to boarding school, which meant I would only work during the holidays.

When I was in matric my father was involved in a terrible car accident. He sustained serious head injuries and remained in hospital for several months. He regained consciousness after the crash, but his head injuries made him unrecognisable. He didn't seem like himself. After some months, we heard that he would be allowed to come home. We went to visit him again, and this time he did seem like himself, though he had lost a lot of weight. He was also able to recognise us. Then, just when we thought he was fine, he experienced complications, got pneumonia and died.

At the time of his accident, he was about to establish a company with some friends, to expand the supermarket and take it to new heights. One of those friends was a neighbour who had a shop in the Ndwedwe district, lived across from our shop and his wife and my mother were good friends. Another member of the team was a lawyer. My mother was well informed about all my father's business dealings. She knew the prospective business partners had not bought and paid for their shares in the new venture. When my father's estate was wound up, I was at university. My mother supported us, paying our fees from the earnings of the shop.

The men who claimed to be business partners of my father began pressuring her to hand over the business to them. She said one of the partners came to the shop, furious at this insolent woman, kicking her and insisting that she give up the business she had built with her husband. My mother decided that the winding up of the estate was taking too long. In 1984, my last year at Turfloop University she sold the shop to a businessman from another township.

After the sale went through she moved out of the neighbourhood. My mother built an entirely new life and has reinvented herself many times since. She joined a multi-level marketing scheme and built a new home on a property my father had bought before he died. She obtained diploma as a beautician and operated a hair and beauty salon, and later she became a very successful estate agent.

She has seen many women derailed by men who come into their lives after their husbands die. Perhaps that was the expectation when my father died, but she remained resolute. Florida Ntombizanele Zondo lost her husband at the age of 44, and continued building her life and her daughters' until she died at the age of 76.

The Secret Pals

I first articulated my dream to fight for justice in 1975, when I applied to do my high school studies at Inanda Seminary. My two sisters were already attending the boarding school and I was extremely excited about joining them. I had applied, submitted a written motivation spelling out why I should be accepted and was called in for an interview. When I returned to the school as a guest speaker many decades later, the student who introduced me at the function said that I had realised my childhood dreams and qualified as a lawyer. She had looked up my school record and discovered the motivation I had submitted in 1975 at the age of eleven, in which I declared that 'I want to be a lawyer, to help people when they are arrested unjustly'.

Attending that school had a major effect on my life. When I arrived, I had the advantage of having older siblings at the school and a sense of the exciting experiences that lay in store for me. I had learned from my sisters that there would be tough times, but overall, it would be an amazing experience. And that is how it turned out. One of the tougher experiences was the initiation practices, the 'hazing' that was a feature of many boarding schools.

Although it was understood that there could be no physical assault of any sort, or interference with private property, initiation caused a serious amount of emotional trauma for some children. During the few months of initiation, all new girls needed someone to protect them. Freshers were afraid to move around the premises on our own. Protectors would be appointed to walk with the fresher on campus.

Even though I had protection, I encountered the ridicule, intimidation and harassment of the initiation practices that took several forms. For example, I was required to sing a song that a senior had made up. 'Mina ngikhala njengo piano' (I sound like the piano) and was repeatedly interrupted when my quivering voice attempted to sing. This did not stop even when I broke down in tears. One day outside the bathrooms, I was required to follow the meaningless instruction to fill my cup, half, with water. Each time I returned with a cup of water – whether filled to the brim or half-filled – the senior rejected my effort.

Initiation was intended to undermine the confidence of freshers by placing them in strange and confusing situations, where they felt completely unsure about what was going to happen to them and unable to do anything about it. I have come to learn that a typical description of trauma is 'encountering devastating danger and being unable to do anything about it'. I found initiation at Inanda Seminary traumatic. Even though I knew that I was in no danger of physical harm from anyone, I did not exercise my autonomy and refuse to carry out instructions from the senior students. Instead of removing myself from the harassment, I suffered helplessly. I have come to learn that remaining in a traumatising situation is a typical trauma response.

My high school years provided me with several deep and enduring friendships. Being among some eighty-five young girls in a grade, living together in dormitories and bearing the lasting identity of being a member (we spelt it 'memba') creates rich and rewarding relationships. Today I still belong to a group of friends originating from Inanda Seminary, and we call ourselves The Secret Pals. It had been in vogue to have pen pals with whom one corresponded by letter. In our classes at Inanda it became the custom to have a secret pal to anonymously take care of you before the reveal happened and names were again picked for a new round of caregiving. We would give each other little gifts to cheer us up. I might open my desk one morning and find a little surprise, a note or a snack – nothing elaborate but always special – bringing joy and excitement and reminding me that I am loved.

After high school our group of Secret Pals grew and developed a new, evolving ethos. We have become a circle of deep love and care, holding each other up through all our experiences. We share the mundane things, the joys, the beauty, the crises and pains of our lives over WhatsApp. We also engage in meaningful conversations about the state of our country and the world and are supportive observers and guides to each other as we navigate positions of responsibility in our professional lives.

Inanda was the first environment where I encountered white people. We had several white teachers and came to regard them as no different to black teachers. We addressed all our male teachers as Baba and all women teachers were called Ma if they were married and Nkosazana if they were single, whether black or white. This approach created a sense that it was unacceptable for people to be treated differently, for any reason. We were all human beings.

Towards the end of our Form 1 (the sixth grade) Mr Askew, a very tall teacher of British origins who carried himself with an air of aloofness and taught at our Secretarial School, experienced our intolerance towards disrespect for blackness. One evening he was on duty during study period. As he neared our class, he must have heard the noise we were making but when he opened the door there was absolute silence and we were all intensely focused on the schoolbooks on our desks. Frustrated because nobody responded to his enquiry about who was making noise during study, his face turned red with anger, and he blurted out the words: 'You mongrels of the third grade!' The whole class rose to their feet, screaming loudly and clasping their hands to the sides of their heads. Within minutes Mr Askew very quickly carried his large body away. While we all were genuinely and deeply saddened by his insults, I broke out in hysterical laughter when my desk mate Gugu Mhlongo, who had given a notable protest performance against Mr Askew, asked, 'what is a mongrel?'

The class filed a formal written complaint against Mr Askew with Miss Gcabashe, who was acting principal at the time. We were never invited to any enquiry process, but Mr Askew soon left the school. We were never told what the reasons were for his departure, but the story that we carried was that racist conduct is unacceptable and never allowed.

Even as teenagers, membas had fully formed political views. We saw it as self-evident that we had a meaningful purpose and equal rights. We looked forward to living in a country that was free of discrimination and where our full potential was realised. Our school ignited in us the passion to honour who we truly are, rallying us around its motto, Shine Where You Are, equipping us with the confidence and ability to speak about our place in the world.

English was the medium of instruction at Inanda. There was a language rule, strictly enforced, that we spoke English from Monday to Friday. There were certain times when we could get away with stolen mother-tongue conversations, but if a prefect found you breaking the language rule, a mark would be placed against your name.

MY RECORD SHOWS THAT I attempted to be a model student. I received punishment for minor infractions only and the punishment was doing chores at weekends. I continued being overly concerned about doing everything right to avoid getting into trouble. I cried while defending myself against the dreaded punishment of getting marked. I was that much of a stickler for the rules. My obedient behaviour earned me a name from our accountancy teacher, Mr Goba. Fascinated by the rather old ways of twelve-year-old me, he began affectionately calling me Aunty Lou and the name survives to this day. Friends from high school and beyond, younger and older, still call me Aunty Lou.

Within the first term of Form 1 my best friend, Xoliswa 'Xoli'

Kakana, and I gained admission into the rather select gymnastic club, the PT Group. Together with Tiny Cele, we were the only Form 1s admitted to the group. Xoli and Tiny excelled at doing handstands, flipping their bodies forward and backwards with ease and graceful agility. Tiny's name spoke truth about the size of her body, she was expert at balancing at the top of the group's three-tier pyramid. The PT Group practised weekly and showcased its abilities at major school events such as the annual speech day, the 'At Home' during visits to the school by distinguished guests and during our visits to other schools. I excelled at doing the splits and balancing positions with my legs folded in the lotus position.

ALTHOUGH MY LIFE AT BOARDING school ranks high on the list of my happiest days, and I thoroughly enjoyed and performed well in academic work, the fear of being on the wrong side of rules remained the dominant driver of my life. I tried to motivate others to be as careful about the rules and etiquette as I was. To this day some of my friends tease me about my reaction when one sunny Saturday afternoon, a fellow dormitory mate removed a blanket from her bed and lay it out on the lawns in front of the Stanwood building (the visitor's reception) to watch the visitors. In shock, I protested that her actions were a disgrace. Everybody who heard that burst out laughing, but I maintained my stance and appealed to them to take the seriousness of the act into account.

Academic excellence was a primary requirement for admission to Inanda and the school expected all of us to maintain our good marks. My parents expected that I would be top of my class from the start, but that was not achievable. In my first year I was often among the top three students in my grade, but in subsequent years I was content with being in the top ten.

Our matric year presented a complex set of obstacles that took many of us decades to overcome – if we ever did. The problem centred around a new principal, Mrs Constance Khoza, who was appointed after the school experienced a series of governance and financial challenges. There had been two principals in the same number of years, notable staff rotation and student discontent and protest for various reasons including bad food. MaKhoza, a memba of the class of '54, was determined to restore Inanda to its glory days with an iron fist. Our clashes with her divided our class and in the second half of our matric year the unity we had thrived on since 1976 crumbled before our eyes.

Some membas in the Class of '80 aligned themselves with MaKhoza, staying in and around her house because they were in danger, because they supported everything that MaKhoza did. Some of the saddest effects of this great rupture in the class of 1980 were that we did not have a proper Matric dance, and my results were badly affected. I could hardly study for the final examinations and my poor results included Cs, Ds and even an E. Relations between the students were in tatters; we could not summon the unity and cooperation required to organise a matric dance. We could not ask MaKhoza to help us plan the dance, resources would not have been made available.

She often would declare, 'Aningazi mina! Ngizonibonisa ukuthi ngingubani! NginguThoko Khoza mina!' (You don't know who I am! I will show you who I am! I'm Thoko Khoza!') She had come to a school where the children were quite liberated, treasured their freedom and were vocal about it, and she sought to bring all into her line. We had a tradition of fixing our uniforms by lifting the skirts up and tucking them under our chins, freeing both hands to pull the shirt down into place. This perfectly innocent act sent MaKhoza into a rage; she accused us of flaunting ourselves in front of everybody. When she passed away in 2017 it was hard for the Class of '80 to pay tribute at MaKhoza's memorial service. When it became obvious that no one was responding to the call for a speaker from our year, I stood up and shared what she had meant to us. I said that she had a complex legacy, particularly for the Class of '80 that experienced her leadership style as authoritarian and confrontational, and resisted it. I shared my views on the dangers of a single story and said that I was glad I had seen the many facets of MaKhoza. I had experienced the compassionate side of MaKhoza on Thursday 17 July 1980, when I was called out of class to go to her house. My sister Jackie was there when

I arrived. MaKhoza came into the room and conveyed to us in the most comforting voice that we had come to an unimaginable point in our lives. She told us that our father had died. She gave us soothing words, which I cannot now remember, prayed with us and sent us home in the school vehicle. I also had the opportunity to warmly love and embrace MaKhoza when I encountered her in the Methodist Women's Manyano (the Methodist Women's Prayer and Service Union). In closing, and to emphasise the sentiment I hold about the unspeakable power of love; I read out 'You and I', a beautiful poem written by one of the most talented poets with South African roots Lebo Mashile.

Hurt people hurt, as they say. But that doesn't mean they cannot also be gentle, nurturing and loving people. The MaKhoza who caused us so much pain was lovingly raising her own grandchildren. They were at school with us, and we showed them our nasty side, vindictively telling them that their grandmother was evil.

My experience with MaKhoza taught me that we are not only one thing. We are many things. It is even true that we are everything.

I declared my intention to become a lawyer as an eleven-year-old child after watching a TV show about a crusading legal eagle. My father was pleased by this prospect and encouraged me to pursue this path. 'When you get your first degree, and you enter your LLB (Bachelor of Laws) studies, I will also enrol for my LLB,' he said. 'And we will work towards completing our law degrees together.'

I regarded attending Inanda Seminary as an important step up the path to lawyering. But the school system seemed far more concerned about producing scientists than lawyers. Inanda selected the top ten students to join the natural sciences stream of physical science and biology. That did not work for me. Heaven knows I tried, but I could not grasp that strange Periodic Table of the Elements. It brought me to tears. I worked hard but I could not understand how protons and electrons combined to create chemical reactions, and how we ended up with H_2O!

Our science teachers insisted that chemistry and physics would give me deeper insights into the natural world and teach me a way of thinking that would serve me well throughout life – even if I became a lawyer. I cried my way out of taking physical science in Form 3 and did history and biology.

Only now, after a long career spent in the practice, creation and application of the law, am I coming to understand the most fundamental nature of the laws of physics and chemistry – the laws of the universe. I am learning that physics, the study of matter and energy, governs the way we interact, our health and wellbeing. It seems that my character and dreams crystallised into my career path. My best friend Xoli is a more sharp-eyed, active and curious person. If a clock broke, she would try to figure out how to fix it. It was obvious that she would become an engineer. My temperament made me a natural fit for law – my empathetic nature, my desire to help people in distress and my obsession with helping others to follow the rules.

My commitment to a career in law came under serious threat when I fell in love during my second year of high school. My boyfriend was studying at Adams College and his dream was to become a doctor. He would visit me during open visiting weekends; there were only four a year. Attending the school's At Home was another opportunity for visits. Most of our relationship was conducted by writing letters and sharing photographs. I was cute and ridiculous. In a state of youthful euphoria, I began to imagine my life with this boyfriend. He would be a doctor and I would work alongside him as a nurse.

On my next visit home, I informed my mother and her cousin Aunt Nomsa Magore, who was visiting from Harare, that I had changed my mind about becoming a lawyer, that I was going to be a nurse. I believed there was a romantic synergy between doctors and nurses, probably something I learned from the plot of a medical drama I may have seen during school movie nights.

Both my mother and Aunt Nomsa were registered nurses and were quite clear that they had all the relevant information and experience to be definitive about not accepting my suggestion of becoming a nurse. They firmly pointed out that I was going to become a lawyer and there was no reason to change that dream.

I could not explain to them why and how I had decided to change my career path. My young mind had been captured by gender stereotyping, which is insidiously channelled into our lives. Thankfully the older and wiser women came to my rescue.

Our parents' rule on boyfriends was that we would not keep them a secret. We were told that the decent thing was to bring them home and introduce them to the family, so they could get to know them. My boyfriend lived in the Eastern Cape, so there wasn't really a chance to have much interaction when I was home during school holidays. He had an aunt in F Section KwaMashu, so we were sometimes able to meet. When I was in Form 3 I told my mother that I had a boyfriend. She chuckled, perhaps in some discomfort and said, 'Oh, puppy love!'.

The pinnacle of social interaction for our school cohort was to go into town for a movie date. Girls who had boyfriends would tell romantic tales of how they had seen a movie and then walked arm-in-arm up West Street. It sounded beautiful. Meanwhile, at our home, we were not allowed to go to town on our own, and we spent all our holidays working at the shop.

But in December 1979, after dating for more than two years, I decided that I was tired of making excuses for being unable to go on a movie date. These would be elaborate, terrible excuses like dumping him at the start of the holidays, so that he would not keep on insisting we should go to the movies. I decided I was going to ask for permission to go on a date with my boyfriend. I postponed asking my parents until it was now or never. On the Thursday before the appointed Saturday, I summoned up the courage and reminded my mother about my boyfriend.

'Yes, I remember,' she said, busying herself with this and that in the kitchen and not looking directly at me.

Leaning against the stove, I said, 'He has asked me to go to the movies with him, in town, on Saturday and I would like to go.'

'Well, you will have to ask Daddy,' she said.

'Okay, good night, Mummy,' I said, and went off to my room, my heart pounding because of this heavy burden.

After supper on Friday night, my father's usual routine consisted of watching the 9pm news on TV, playing hymns on the organ, stretching himself out of the organ stool, going to his bedroom and emerging in his bathrobe, humming a song. I interrupted his routine while he was stretching on the organ stool.

'Daddy, I want to tell you that I have a boyfriend,' I said, trying hard not to allow any hesitation in my voice.

'Oh, who is he?' my father asked in a tone I could not quite assess.

'His name is Themba.'

After responding to further questions about where he was from and whose child he was, I put my request to my father without pausing for breath. 'Themba asked me to go to the movies in town with him tomorrow. He is visiting his aunt at F Section. I would like to have your permission to go with him to town.'

He rose from the stool and sent me to bed, without giving me an answer. I bade him goodnight and did as he said.

I had done it! Goodness, I had got it off my chest and asked the question. When I got to our room, Tandi and Jackie were waiting to hear how the conversation had gone. I was so pleased that I slept peacefully that night.

I hung around my father the next morning, waiting for his decision. But he left the house without saying anything. With the date mere hours away, I became frantic. I went to my mother and told her that the movie was starting at 1pm and I had to catch the noon train at Thembalihle station.

'I asked Daddy, but I don't yet have a response! I would like to go.'

'So, you asked him,' she replied. 'Did he say no?'

'No, he didn't say no.'

'Okay, then go.'

In the days before cell phones, appointments were cast in stone. If people agreed to meet at the train station at noon they needed to be there on time as there would be no way of communicating changes to arrangements. Thembalihle Station was less than two kilometres from our house, and I ran all the way and made it on time. Themba and I caught the matinee at the Shah Jehan in Grey Street and went for a fruit cocktail at the Golden Peacock on Victoria Street. We promenaded down West Street arm-in-arm. I wanted to make sure we were seen outside Garlick's and the OK Bazaars, an important dating ritual of the time that made it official that Themba and I were a couple.

I returned home in good time before dark. Jackie was waiting for me at the gate and anxiously told me that my father had asked where I was. I explained that I had permission from our mother, no refusal from our father and gave her a blow-by-blow account of my day. I was the first among my siblings to confess to having a boyfriend while we were still living at home. I paved the way for my older sisters to act on the uncomfortable house rule of reporting our dating status to the parents. I began to understand that while I may have been the quiet sister, I am also strong and brave. I understood the rules, but I could also see how they could work in my favour. My quiet defiance would come out in various ways throughout my life.

By the middle of the matric year, university applications were due. I applied to the University of Natal but, as a black person, I could not automatically gain admission into this university designated for whites. I applied for permission from the Minister of Internal Affairs stating that I wished to enrol to study forensic medicine as part of my law degree. It wasn't offered a place at any of the black universities and I was confident that permission would be granted. Much to my dismay, the Minister of Internal Affairs responded that he was glad to advise that with effect from January 1980, forensic medicine would be offered at the University of Fort Hare and I was free to apply there without any need for ministerial permission.

I sought advice from Uncle Justice Moloto, a practising lawyer at the time. (He was appointed as a judge at the International Criminal Tribunal for the former Yugoslavia in The Hague.) Uncle Justice and Aunt Vuyelwa were married and lived in D Section, Umlazi. Aunt Vuyelwa (Dr Mashalaba) had lived in our home while she was at medical school, so we considered her family. Without promising much prospect of success, Uncle Justice drafted a letter of appeal on several grounds, including that the forensic medicine department was newly established at Fort Hare and I had missed their application deadlines. The Minister of Internal Affairs would not budge. At the end of 1980 I realised, with a shock, that my dream of becoming a lawyer was slipping from my grasp. Several of my friends were in a similar boat.

Our parents got together. One of them discovered that Turfloop (the University of the North) was accepting applications in person, and they arranged that we all travel there in time for the start of orientation week for new students. A group of about eight young isiZulu-speaking women were put onto a train at Durban station and sent off to begin our adult lives in a part of the country we had never been to before. Most of us had never heard anyone speak TshiVenda, SePedi or XiTsonga. We arrived in Pietersburg at 4am. Taxis got us to the gates of the Turfloop campus at 7am. We were filled with the excitement of adventure. Our in-person applications were all accepted and our student careers began.

I was still in a relationship with Themba, my first boyfriend. But I was also rolling into my adult life and that would prove to be a completely different country. My qualities of shy courage and defiant compliance with the rules expressed themselves again during my first year of university when I met a man eight years older.

He was quite dazzling, well known on campus, the chairperson of the Central Cultural Committee with the custody of the keys to all its assets. This included the music system, all the records and other equipment. He pursued me and eventually I agreed to explore a relationship with him. I was a fresh-faced seventeen-year-old. After the night I ended up in his room in the men's section on campus, I came back to my room, sat down at my desk and I wrote a letter to my mother: 'Yesterday, I went to a man's room. I ended up spending the night with him, and we had sexual intercourse.'

My mother wrote back, thanking me for letting her know about the developments in my life. She offered advice: 'I hope you will go to the clinic and collect contraceptives to prevent pregnancy.' Years later I asked my mother how she felt when she received that letter. 'Yes, of course I was shocked,' she said. 'It was hard to bear, but it was exactly what I had wished for. It reassured me to know that you were not going into excessive danger, that you were trying to make the best of the freedom that you had, in being away from home. But you were still staying connected to us, and our values.'

I didn't follow her advice. In December 1982, the end of my second year at university, I returned home to Durban and realised that I had missed my period. I broke the news to my mother just as she was relaying something about her best friend's daughter.

Returning from her visit to Mrs Bolani in F Section, she told me, 'My friend was devastated! Her daughter returned home from university and reported that she was pregnant. I had to encourage my friend, and tell her, it's not the end of the world. We can support the child. She can have the baby, and she can be supported to build her life and fulfil her dreams…'

'It's funny you should say that,' I interrupted my mother. 'Because I think I also haven't had my period and I'm beginning to suspect I might also be pregnant.'

That's how my firstborn son Sheikani enters my story.

The Turfloop upheaval

Why did I write a letter to my mother telling her about the first time I had sex? I have asked myself this question many times since then and settled on an interpretation which came from the responses of friends when I told them what I had done. It was a confusing experience, I did not know how to make sense of it and my mother was the only person I could speak to, in the circumstances.

The group of young girls from Durban who had travelled to the heart of the far Northern Transvaal stuck together through the many wild parties of orientation week and the start of our academic programmes. A hostel room, VG123, became our hangout. We built a strong identity on campus, vibrant young girls from Inanda Seminary who became a curiosity. We were also something of an annoyance, with our loud Zulu conversation, free-spirited laughter and our propensity for raucous fun. Unfortunately, the hostel matron's suite was right next door to VG123, and often she would emerge from her quarters shouting: 'Ke bomang bao ba dirago lešata!' (Who is making that noise!) The hostel seniors would respond in a denigrating way, 'Ke MaZulunyana leMaThosanyana ao, Matron.' (It's those little Zulus and Xhosas, Matron.)

We would return from lectures and go straight to our room in Vrouens Slaapsaal Blok G Kamer 123. The door was always open, and there was always someone with whom to shoot the breeze. I was not the first among the VG123 friends to have a boyfriend. Penny had one and was generous enough to advise that spending the night at the men's hostel was not a challenge at all. She told me that she felt very safe and comfortable sleeping over in her boyfriend's room because she did not remove her jeans.

The subject came up after her first night away from the women's hostel because Penny and I had expressed intentions of not having sex before we were twenty-one. I turned seventeen in February 1981 and Penny was turning seventeen in July. When I started dating Sheiks Makhado in March, I was not worried at all about the risk of sex. Penny's experience had set my mind at ease.

A shortcoming though was that I wore a long multi-coloured skirt on my Friday evening date with my new boyfriend. Another mistake, as Penny would subsequently make a point of reminding me, was expecting my boyfriend to be gentle. When we got to Sheiks' room in Men's Block F, relying on the protection of my beige full-slip petticoat was futile. Apparently, a full slip can't match the chastity-preserving power of a pair of jeans!

After the act, I couldn't decipher my feelings. I gathered the blood-stained sheets from Sheiks' bed and placed them in a plastic bag with the intention of washing them at my hostel. Nobody had asked me to do this, but this is what I did. It was around noon when we walked back to my hostel, chatting easily.

I went straight to my room on the second floor, sat quietly at my desk and wrote that famous letter to my mother. That done, I walked to the post office just outside the university gates and slipped the sealed, stamped envelope into the red post box. After my first encounter with sex, I struggled to form a coherent story describing what had happened. I was embarrassed about not following the established route of keeping one's jeans on. I did not know how I felt about breaking my promise to not have sex before the age of twenty-one. I had a lump of ambivalence in my heart.

I found myself in circumstances that had developed beyond my control. Even though I did not have the language at that time, I bore disquiet in my body.

I was carrying something traumatic, and my mother was the only person with whom I could share it. I employed this angle when sharing the experience with my girlfriends in VG123. I could focus on the fact that I had written to my mother about it, and not that I was rather traumatised by the way I had sex for the first time. The letter became something of a punchline, which was helpful during my process of dealing with the trauma through avoidance.

I never took to VG123 the incidents of violence and assault that followed. I had never been assaulted by a boyfriend before. My friends and I considered such behaviour unacceptable and intolerable. Sheiks first assaulted me in my room at VG205. He kicked me and I fell, knocking the back of my knee against a metal chair. The bruise from that injury hardened into scar tissue that I carried for a long time. I never told my friends about the abuse or the fear it created. Although I became afraid of Sheiks, I did not end the relationship. I became docile and quiet around him, always uncertain about what might anger him and possibly trigger a violent reaction. I used moodiness as a form of protection against outbursts. I never mentioned the assaults to anyone or the outbursts that were just as abusive. I silently hid the humiliation it caused.

Only in recent years – inspired by young women speaking out against misogyny, rape culture and all forms of violence against women and gender non-binary people at tertiary institutions, particularly in the context of the FeesMustFall movement – have I poured out these truths to my friends. I came to realise that many of them had similar violent experiences and had suffered silently. My heart feels crushed by the reality that young women at tertiary education institutions still experience the same violence we endured decades ago. Despite our deep anger and frustration at the unabating violence against women, we lack the kind of systemic change required to shift society away from gender-based violence.

I must have fallen pregnant around October of my second

year at university, because it was in December that I came to my mother with the news that I thought I was expecting. We went to a doctor and the pregnancy test was positive. My mother was completely supportive. I returned to university at the beginning of the next year.

South Africa was in the throes of violent upheaval as police brutality intensified in the face of growing solidarity against apartheid. The launch of the United Democratic Front in 1983 under the slogan UDF Unites, Apartheid Divides was momentous, as it mobilised the largest range of civil society organisations across the country in a single structure. One of the UDF's goals was to resist the Tricameral Parliament system in which the South African government sought to introduce racially divided legislatures for Indian, Coloured and white people. In its grand scheme the apartheid regime orchestrated the erasure of black people from South Africa by designating them citizens of the ten ethnically defined self-governing or independent homelands. The relentless determination of the anti-apartheid forces to render the country ungovernable eventually contributed to the overthrow of the regime.

Turfloop, like many other education institutions, was a site of struggle, and protests against the apartheid authorities were met with brutal police and army attacks on students. Around the end of May 1983, my third year of study, riots broke out on campus and the university was closed before the end of the first semester examinations.

I had moved out of the hostel and was living in Sheiks' parental home in Mankweng, the residential area that was home to many university professionals. Sheiks' father was a senior lecturer at Turfloop. I returned home to Durban on 15 June, when the birth was imminent. With a doctor's certificate confirming that it was safe for me to be on the flight, I managed to fly from Pietersburg to Durban even though I was at an advanced stage of pregnancy. The stress of commuting the thousand-odd kilometres from Pietersburg to Durban by bus, train or taxi would have been out of the question.

Sheikani was born on 27 June 1983 at St Aidan's Hospital. My mother took me to a gynaecologist, Dr Foster, who admitted me around 1pm. By 4pm the intensity of the labour pains was unbearable and Dr Foster ordered an epidural. Around 8pm I woke up from sleep, feeling an overwhelming urge to use the toilet.

'Please bring me the bedpan,' I politely asked the nursing staff. 'I need to relieve myself.'

'We're waiting for your doctor,' one of the nurses replied.

It was torture. Nurses can be overwhelmed and impatient at times, so I beseeched them with all the humility and politeness I could muster, to please bring the bedpan. They ignored me completely.

Finally, the doctor arrived. It turned out that I was absolutely ready to give birth and had perhaps not needed the bathroom after all. The gut-wrenching exertions of the birth were soon over, and it was the most amazing experience to hold my first child in my arms. Sheikani emerged with a fatty coating on his skin, particularly across his chubby little face. I was told it is vernix caseosa, or birthing custard, and that it was an extremely good sign as the fat would protect and nourish his skin. I surrendered to the amazing, overwhelming experience of being a mother to Sheikani.

He weighed a healthy 3.8kg. In a spirit of supreme elation, I returned to my mother's house. While the lead-up to the birth had essentially gone according to expectations, the post-partum period was extremely difficult. On Sheikani's third day, I suddenly found myself unable to cope. My mother came home in the middle of the morning to find both baby and mother wailing. I was feverish and almost delirious with pain and frustration. I was unable to feed Sheikani. My breasts had become engorged and unbearably painful. I couldn't take my baby's crying and was slipping into depression. Fortunately, my mother was a nurse. She heated cloths, placed them on my breasts and helped me to express milk. My temperature went down and my mother attended to the baby who slowly began suckling, putting us all at ease.

In the way of many of life's most visceral moments, the period of birth is an incredibly delicate balance. When one of the many elements needed to sustain life and health becomes disturbed, things slip out of focus. One imbalance creates another, and a new mother's physical and mental wellbeing can quickly be disturbed. Within three days of giving birth, I felt overwhelmed by the many demands of parenting. There was always a bucket of cloth nappies that needed washing and bottles that needed to be washed, sterilised and filled. I had been given an episiotomy during the birth process, so going to the bathroom was agony. I wanted to cover the stitches with my hand every time I went to relieve myself. The pressures that single mothers are forced to deal with are quite unbearable, and I found myself buckling under the strain.

When my grandchildren were born, I made a point of insisting that I would be there for the birth, and that I would provide all the support I could to the parents – the mothers specifically. No woman wants to be seen as a bad mother, so we try to manage everything on our own. Looking after a baby has always been a shared responsibility and an exercise in mutual support. No one should be expected to bear such a heavy load on their own. It was particularly important to me to spend a lot of time with my grandchildren from the time they were born. I gave myself permission to be a full-time grandmother, which meant my own twin stroller when Mia and Maik were born five months apart, my own booster car seats and stock of baby food. When my grandchild Kaya was born in 2018, I moved into his parents' home to assist with caring for mother and child.

When Sheikani was five days old his father arrived from Pietersburg. He had hitch-hiked to Durban. I have never seen so much excitement. Sheiks seemed to be jumping up and down the whole day at the sight of the baby, his son! Then he told me that he would be going home the next day and suggested that we get married before he left. I was in such a daze that I didn't think the idea through. It seemed to follow that because we had a baby, we should get married. We went into town and purchased a wedding ring at a Game store. It looked gold-plated, and it had a heart design. My mother insisted on an antenuptial contract, but Sheiks disagreed and after a consultation with a lawyer he did not change his mind.

'We are getting married,' he said. 'We are getting married on the basis that we want to build together. Why are you already looking at a dissolution? Why is everybody concentrating on the dissolution of this partnership? I am not getting married in order to be divorced. So, we are not going to sign an antenuptial contract.'

Unable to assert myself with any conviction in the midst of my post-partum confusion, I simply shrugged, and we returned to KwaMashu to be married at the G3 Methodist Church. We needed a witness, and the person working in the kitchen was called in to assist. The minister solemnised the marriage and after a couple of minutes the formalities were completed. I couldn't control the giggles that came over me. As so often happens in the face of a surreal situation, all I could do was laugh.

Towards the end of July 1993 I returned to Turfloop with Sheikani and continued to live with Sheiks' family while I completed a deferred exam and continued my studies. My results were some of the best I achieved, thanks to my sheer joy and sense of purpose. I was bonding with Sheikani while I was studying, with him snugly asleep on my lap as I did my reading. I dared not move, because the minute he stirred, his grandmother would appear and insist that he come to her, to prevent disturbing my studies.

Young mother, young student

My campus image had transformed radically from strait-laced young person to heavily pregnant mother-to-be sporting enormous tent dresses as I waddled between lectures. I was pleasantly surprised when, a month after Sheikani's birth, I was able to fit into my normal clothes with greater ease than before my pregnancy. It turned out that the loss of youthfulness was temporary.

I was grateful for the support I had throughout my pregnancy. In 1983, the lives of many VG123 friends had taken them to different medical schools, other universities and training institutions. But those who remained at Turfloop habitually stopped by at Sheiks' home to visit me on their frequent visits to Tinties, the local supermarket. I was supported on campus by my classmate Susan Masapu, who lured me to her hostel room under the pretext of study sessions, when she wanted to provide me with a place to rest between lectures. Susan often shared her hostel lunches with me, and I was deeply grateful for her loving kindness.

My sister Jackie, who had been deeply hurt and challenged by the news of my pregnancy, became a doting aunt to Sheikani. Jackie left Turfloop after her second year and was studying at the University of Zululand, Ongoye, when Sheikani was born, but she remained very present to me. My sister Tandi maintained her gentle, loving character and could not contain her excitement at becoming an aunt. There were many times when I would walk into the room and find my mother staring at Sheikani in his sleep with a beaming smile across her face. She was fascinated by this beautiful baby as she only had experience of baby girls. Sheiks continued to dote over Sheikani while his family provided me with generous support, allowing me to concentrate on my academic work and providing space for social interaction when I needed it. I was treated as a daughter in the family, rather than a makoti whose primary duty was to serve the Makhado family, as tradition would have it for many.

Sheikani became the light in my life, and I felt privileged to be raising him. He was 18 months old when I completed the BProc in December 1984 and returned to Durban to enrol at the University of Natal for my Bachelor of Laws (LLB) studies. It was a hard transition, as the course load was exponentially heavier than I had experienced at Turfloop. Sheikani's father had stayed behind in the north and was teaching in Venda. I was again living in my mother's house in D Section, KwaMashu. I used public transport to get to university, which meant leaving my mother's house every morning at dawn, walking to the station, taking a minibus taxi to town, getting off on Ridge Road (now called Peter Mokaba Ridge Road), and walking 4km up the steep incline of King George V Avenue (now called Mazisi Kunene Road) to get to Howard College, the law school, for my first lecture.

If I was lucky, someone would stop to offer me a lift to campus. Apartheid spatial planning, among other things, assumed the luxury of private transport in areas designated as white suburbs and made no provision for public transport. In the afternoons I would grapple with having to use the library after my lectures while transport from the university to KwaMashu and other townships became rarer than hen's teeth. On days when I was stranded on campus after dark, I would hike a lift to the Warwick Road bus terminus in town, take the Ntuzuma bus and get off at the KwaMashu train station, where I would catch the local minibus taxi to Sigwegwe Road, D Section and walk up the 800m to my mother's home.

I made sure that I collected as much of the material I needed from the library during the day, using the breaks between my lectures, so that I had no need to stay late on campus. I made friends who formed my study support network whether they knew it or not. Ray Zondo, now Chief Justice of South Africa, was a pillar of strength. We were enrolled for the LLB at the same time. He already had a wealth of experience with law from serving articles at the firm of anti-apartheid struggle stalwarts Griffiths and Victoria Mxenge, who were murdered in 1981 and 1985 respectively, because of their political activism. Ray supported me quite a lot – especially with his study notes.

I soon realised that I had not gained a universally admired qualification when I earned my BProc from Turfloop. Not without some justification, the university was regarded as an academic backwater, staffed in the main by third-grade Afrikaner academics. They lazily taught from study guides and would fail students for applying their minds beyond the guides and offering views arising from other sources. For our Afrikaner lecturers at Turfloop, not only was it too much of an effort to consider arguments of any sort, but it was also their appointed duty – by all means available – to limit the capacities of the intelligentsia emerging from Turfloop. This was in line with the Verwoerdian philosophy of confining black people to being hewers of wood and carriers of water for the benefit of white domination.

In my transfer for the LLB degree, the University of Natal did not grant me credit for my Turfloop majors, and I had to repeat seven of the courses I had passed in my first degree. I cried because the herculean efforts of my widowed mother, who single-handedly gathered the financial and other resources to see me through a four-year degree (while financing my siblings' education as well), was devalued by the requirement that I repeat so many courses. I cried because I felt the blind arrogance of our education system which was so steeped in inequality. The University of Natal proclaimed itself superior and made no attempt to assess the students qualifying from institutions like Turfloop. I cried because while at Turfloop, I had missed out on the vibrancy of discourse taking place in the lecture rooms of the University of Natal. Nazeer Cassim's teaching of labour law and Nic Rycroft's delivery of race legislation challenged us. Advocate Louis Skweyiya jostled us into reimagining the offences of treason and sedition by questioning whether it was feasible for these crimes to be committed in circumstances where the state's legitimacy and authority were contested in national and international law.

I stuck to my task with all the help I could grab. I updated my knowledge and pulled together the confidence to engage in arguments with people who so eloquently debated the disconnects and intersections between positive law and natural law theories and quoted social contract theorists such as Thomas Hobbes, John Locke and Jean-Jacque Rousseau on their contribution to the evolution of natural law. Inevitably, I constantly confronted the inner judge in me who, erroneously, advised me to silence my voice. I had regular crises of confidence in the company of confident young people at Howard College who debated issues at dinner tables with elders in the high echelons of the country's legal, judicial, economic and political circles.

My inner critic presented itself as a wise counsel protecting me from being exposed and embarrassed because of the shortcomings of my late and disadvantaged start on the journey to obtaining the LLB degree from Howard College. I quite frequently battled anxiety as the inner judge demeaned the value of my capacities and contributions, and suggested that my achievements were a result of external factors including luck. This is similar to what is known in psychology as imposter syndrome or perceived fraudulence. But slowly, gradually, I gained confidence and made the imposter syndrome stand down. I was among the top four finalists in our final-year Moot Court programme, and this inspired me and filled me with joy and gratitude.

I have struggled with building my confidence throughout my life. From an early age, I battled with imposter syndrome. At Ekusizaneni Higher Primary School I would be called out of my class by teachers of more senior classes, who would ask me to stand in front of their students and answer questions. This performance was psychologically damaging. Mr Khumalo, a teacher of the seventh year of school, was particularly fond of this demonstration. The students in his class were around thirteen years old and I was ten.

'Even she knows the answers,' he would say. 'You are being beaten by a little child!'

The prospect of getting the question wrong would frighten me to a state of breathlessness. Yet, I outwardly maintained my composure. I was deadly afraid of conflict with children, especially girls. I stood in front of the class tortured by thoughts of them harassing and bullying me in retaliation for the humiliation to which Mr Khumalo had subjected them. As I stood there paralysed by apprehension but mechanically delivering the correct answers, it must have looked like arrogance. Had there been some praise for me, some acknowledgement that I was the clever one it might have been worth it, but I did not feel any. All I felt was something breaking inside.

At the end of the academic year the school would hold a special assembly, where the principal announced the top achievers in each grade. Other children were thrilled when their names were called, they jumped off the veranda and trotted joyfully across the quad to accept the cheers of their schoolmates. But that was the last thing I wanted. I would break inside. I would literally be falling to pieces inside from the shyness. As I walked to the front, my movements were slow. I couldn't trust my legs to carry me to the principal's podium, I was scared I would trip and fall in front of the whole school. One of the teachers told my mother she had interpreted my slow walk as a level of self-assuredness that she had never witnessed in one so young. Fortunately, my mother knew me well and laughed it off.

I was anxious when I succeeded and when I failed. I was bad at reciting poetry and memorised passages. I was shy, so I was terrible when performing. My anxiety was crippling. Sometimes I would be overcome by shyness when raising my hand to answer a teacher's question. I would become frozen with fear when I had to speak. Often the teacher would then call on someone else and I would mutter beneath my breath, 'I knew that. I knew that. I knew that too!'

That was sometimes interpreted as arrogance. But it was a lack of confidence and it remained in place through all the stages of my life. I often struggle to complete projects, especially when working on my own, or I procrastinate. This dates back to my early days of being anxious about complying with the many home rules, and my school days. Somewhere inside me, even when I am acknowledged for major achievements, there is a contrary voice inside that says, 'They don't know, but that's not true about you. And you just may get exposed any time now…'

During my early days in F section, KwaMashu, I developed a strong desire to not stand out, to not be different, because being pointed out was real torture. Paradoxically, I also wanted to achieve. I wanted to please my parents and meet their requirements. I was aware of the standards that were set and I didn't want to fail. I wanted to make my family proud, I wanted to see the joy on the faces of my father and my mother. But I didn't want it in public. I didn't want it in front of other people.

There was one time where I felt the need to cause a spectacle and correct something that was plainly wrong. It was in Standard Five. The year was 1975, and the curriculum had recently changed. For the first time, all our subjects were being taught in English. An extremely beautiful teacher was teaching us health studies. Aunt Vuyelwa Mashalaba was living with us while she studied medicine and her reference books were all over the house. I would often page through those volumes, discovering new things about the human body and our anatomy. When our teacher instructed us in English about the digestive system, she said that when we eat, our food travels down the 'oiusfungus'.

I knew the correct term and pronunciation was oesophagus. I had to correct the teacher because if she taught us oiusfungus and we were tested, everyone would be wrong. I raised my hand.

'Please Miss, it's oesophagus!'

She completely ignored me.

It was easier to get away with such inaccuracies in those days, because we didn't have the health textbook for our classes. What the teacher taught was the way it was!

Rikhado

I yearned for a second baby soon after Sheikani reached toddlerhood, while I was completing my LLB. Every time I saw a young mother or baby I was drawn towards them. As a child, when my sisters were fighting with me and ignoring me, I resolved that I would have about twelve children. I wanted a huge kitchen table that could seat my children and all their friends. I told Sheiks about my plans and we went to see a doctor to seek assurance that there were no obstacles to us falling pregnant again. The doctor's tests showed no impediments to conception, and he advised that state of mind had a lot to do with success; it helped if the mother was completely stress free – under no pressure and not anxious about making a baby. I took the doctor's advice, relaxed into the process and we eventually became pregnant in 1986.

    I was in a state of bliss for the duration of the pregnancy. I glowed with joy. Eating plenty of avocado pears seemed to add harmony to the experience. Until Rikhado was born on 20 July 1987, I went to work every day with the biggest smile on my face – even after the morning rush of my commute that included taking

Sheikani to pre-school in the Musgrave area. I was filled with love for every aspect of life. I walked down the streets of Durban eating avocado pears that I bought from a fruit-and-vegetable store at the corner of St Andrews (now Diakonia Avenue) and Grey Streets (now Dr Yusuf Dadoo Street), a few metres from work in the Diakonia Building. I mastered the art of neatly removing the avocado peel in a single spiral and as I bit into the delectable fruit I savoured every morsel.

My supportive colleagues at the Legal Resources Centre embraced my pregnancy. I had the good fortune of four months of maternity leave that started two weeks before my due date. Before my confinement I planned to relax for a few weeks before the birth, but that was not to be. My entrepreneurial mother was running a beauty salon in town. I woke up early one Saturday morning to assist her at the salon. Around lunchtime, I noticed that my arm had swelled up alarmingly. It was getting thicker, assuming a darker colour and throbbing. Pulsating! My mother rushed me to McCord Hospital, where I had been born, and many of the pivotal events in my life happened. I was admitted immediately. I was diagnosed with pre-eclampsia. The medical team was unable to bring my blood pressure down over the next three days and decided to induce the birth.

Sheikani had been born at a private hospital with a gynaecologist in private practice in attendance. I had not enjoyed the experience because the nurses had been unwilling to assist with pain relief until my doctor arrived. For the birth of my second child, I promised myself that I would not subject myself to that. I decided I would rely on the support of professionals in the public healthcare system. But again I did not receive the standard-service package for which I had signed up. A group of trainee nurses from St Augustine's – the private hospital generally regarded at the time as a white hospital – had come to McCord to complete their practical studies. As my time approached, this gaggle of white nurses in the maternity ward were even more stressed than I was and suggested several odd interventions to ease my impending delivery.

'Breathe!' I was told. 'Breathe in, breathe out! That's it! Try putting your hands above your head. Why don't you come and sit in this wicker chair? Would you like a massage?' I liked the attention, but it was not quite what I had wanted. I expected a public ward, a doctor on duty who served all the patients and a natural childbirth. What I received was an excessive fussing which did not relieve the pain.

After five hours of labour, my patience ran out and these professionals were no longer my friends. I had changed my mind about the epidural, I was ready for that anaesthesia, pronto. I was told that it was far too late for an epidural. But would I like a hot or cold compress or a foot massage? I was not interested. Eventually, Rikhado was ready to come into the world. The compresses were applied, the nurses massaged. We pushed, and Rikhado was born. The first person to see my newborn son was my sister Jackie's boyfriend Bonga Mfeka. The nurse exponents of the organic approach to childbirth thought Bonga was the father, invited him into the delivery room and handed baby Rikhado to him, covered in the lubrication from my womb.

Four-year-old Sheikani came to visit us at the hospital soon after the birth. Rikhado was the first newborn he had seen and his pallor made a major impression. At home in KwaMashu, he proclaimed that 'uRikhado uwumlungu'. Newborn African babies can be exceptionally light skinned, with hair quite sleek and soft. What, after all, constitutes a white person anyway? 'My brother is going to be a white person,' Sheikani said. 'I'm not, but he's going to be white.'

Some twenty-seven years later, when Rikhado's son Maik was born in Johannesburg, my son was with his partner Bianca in the delivery room and was actively involved. Afterwards, trying not to laugh because it hurt her sutures, Bianca told me that Rikhado had expressed both love and pity for his son. Because of Maik's light complexion at birth, he assumed his baby had albinism.

When Rikhado was born Sheiks and I were renting a flat in Overport, where I established a routine with my baby. My family came to visit regularly, allowing me to rest and heal. One thing I had not bargained for, which I learned is quite natural, was the pain associated with my womb contracting back into place and shrinking to its normal size. I had not experienced that after Sheikani's birth, but I had excruciating abdominal pain when Rikhado suckled at my breast.

Raising two children occupied all my time. At first, their father was hardly present and I did not notice. I was engrossed in being a mother to my children. They took up every space in me. I loved taking them to my mother's home and to my sister..

Sheikani used to express himself by crying. He did so often and could go on for a long time.

'Sheikani,' I would respond. 'It doesn't help to cry. Use your words. What do you want?'

He would continue crying, but it did not annoy me. People around us would get exasperated, but besides odd moments of impatience, I was able to remain philosophical about his bouts of tears. I had a deep connection with my children and I loved every minute with them – whether they were crying or not.

A watershed

The final year of my LLB was in 1986, and I applied for a twelve-month fellowship at the Legal Resources Centre (LRC) in Durban. I had applied to do articles at a few white law firms, but I was afraid of working there. While engaging with jurisprudence and the place of law in society I had allowed myself to be sufficiently troubled by the question: 'How do we practise law in an unjust legal system and still keep our life force?' Fortunately, I was called for an interview at the LRC and offered their fellowship. I welcomed the opportunity of gaining exposure to public interest law. When I began my fellowship, I was pregnant with my second child.

My new colleagues embraced me and my pregnancy. I was given four months of paid maternity leave. I subsequently learned that my leave application had been approved in error and out of policy. The director of the centre was on sabbatical when it was approved, and I was grateful for this administrative error.

Sheiks and I had applied for a British Council fellowship to pursue studies for master's degrees in the United Kingdom. We were both called in for interviews. Although I was pregnant when

I was interviewed, I was awarded the fellowship while he was not. It would enable me to complete a master's degree in human rights law, and I was admitted to the London School of Economics and Political Science for their programme. Because the fellowship was starting in the middle of the year in 1988, the LRC generously invited me to stay on for another six months. This enabled me to continue to earn a livelihood while gaining further experience in the field of human rights law.

Things were coming to a head in my marriage. It was hard for Sheiks to watch me making plans to go to the UK, as the vision had been for us to go together. A streak of jealousy appeared, amidst the tension of being unsure what my departure would mean for us. His jealousy came out in bouts of what I considered ridiculous paranoia. He became obsessed with why a male colleague at the LRC had walked me to the car when he came to collect me at work. I came across photos of a woman that he was keeping. I confronted him about them, and he claimed the woman had sent them completely unsolicited. I told my sister, who was not surprised and who accused me of not listening when I was told my husband was cheating.

I used to rationalise Sheiks' absences when he disappeared on me. The man was involved in the struggle. He had to travel a lot, have meetings with many people. But now the full truth of his infidelity struck home. I realised that he had been carrying on with people known to both of us at university. I felt thoroughly humiliated because everybody knew, while I was the oblivious fool. My supposed friends had been aware all along that he was betraying our relationship.

Soon afterwards, there was another incident. Sheiks was again sparked by his insecurity about my fidelity. He accused me of having had sex with other men after he observed vaginal discharge in the underwear I removed when I got into bed. He began beating me.

'You are my wife,' he screamed as he rained blows on me.

'Not from today,' I replied. 'Know that I am not your wife from this day!'

The captions for these photographs appear on page 163 at the back of the book.

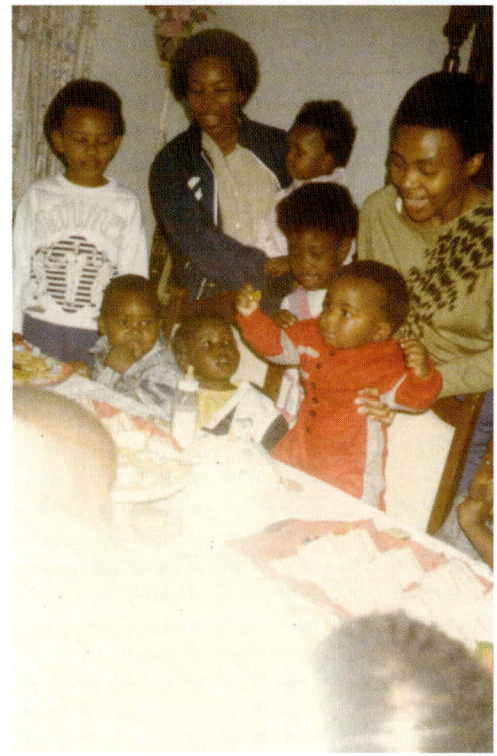

That was the end of it. I decided that I would see out my time at the LRC until August, then leave for the UK. I continued to live with him under the same roof in our rental home in D Section, KwaMashu, even though the relationship was effectively over. My mother agreed that it was pointless to disrupt things too much.

I cut myself off from Sheiks. I no longer cooked for him or attended to him in any way. For the first time, I began knitting. I found a pattern in a magazine, bought balls of wool and began making a jersey. That meant I could sit alone without having to speak to anyone, least of all Sheiks. We had already agreed that Rikhado, who had turned one on 20 July 1988, would remain with his father's family in Mankweng, Turfloop, after my departure. Sheikani, who was five years old, would remain with his father in KwaZulu-Natal, where Sheiks would ensure that he spent time with my mother.

The day of my departure drew near. The atmosphere at home grew ever more toxic. Eventually the tension broke in a bloody, messy assault. It was a Sunday. My sister and I had been out and about, distributing invitations to my farewell party that was to take place the following Friday at my mother's house. I came home and went to bed.

Sheiks must have heard about the party from someone. He arrived home when I was fast asleep and aggressively demanded sex. He was determined to get it, even when I made it clear that was never going to happen. He began beating me. He hit me on the top of my head, so hard that I could immediately taste blood at the back of my throat. I realised I was in trouble. I managed to leave the bedroom and tried to get out of the house, but he followed me. He caught up with me in the kitchen.

I grabbed the nearest weapon, a long, sharp-pointed, serrated knife I had recently bought that was drying on the dish rack on the sink. Without a word, I turned on him and inserted the knife wherever it landed on his body. As he grabbed hold of me, I realised that I needed to hold on to the knife by all means possible, otherwise that might be the death of me. In the struggle for the knife, I bent the stainless-steel knife while holding both handle and sharp blade in my right hand. Sheiks must have felt weak from the bleeding because he let go and called for help from a neighbour who drove him to hospital. I later found out that he was taken to McCord Hospital.

Growing up in KwaMashu, one hears a lot about stabbing. A hand gesture with a limp wrist described the act of stabbing someone. Having seen this in the area, I thought that was how you stabbed somebody. In fear of my life, I stabbed Sheiks again and again. Fortunately, my silly technique only caused several bloody, but minor surface wounds.

After Sheiks was taken to hospital I slowly and methodically cleaned the blood from the carpets and the surfaces of our home while I waited for the sun to come up, so I could go to my mother's house. The kids were asleep. The wind blew throughout the night. When the sun rose, I gathered the kids and went to my mother's home. I told her what had happened. This was the end of things. My mother's best friend was a matron at McCord Hospital. She later told my mother that Sheiks had told her I had tried to kill him.

Later that day I had a consultation with Ray Zondo. I told him that I needed to air all my dirty laundry and gave him instructions to file for divorce. My mother reported the violence to my uncle in the Eastern Cape. Mr Canca, affectionately known as Uncle RS, was a lawyer. He proposed that I leave the country for the UK immediately, preferably on the next flight.

Uncle RS arranged for me to stay with a friend. Mr Livingston Mqotsi was an educator, author, editor and lawyer who had fled South Africa in 1964 and settled in London. Uncle RS made all the arrangements. I would stay with the Mqotsi family for two weeks until my fellowship in London officially started and I could move into university accommodation.

My life changed irrevocably. The assault happened on a Sunday and I was out of the country by the Wednesday. I left Rikhado, who was 14 months old, and Sheikani, who was five years old. By the time Sheiks was discharged from hospital, I was gone.

London calling

After my maternity leave came to an end, I had returned to the Legal Resources Centre. The fellowship in London was drawing near, but the assault and bloody fight at our home meant I had to leave at short notice. I had already planned to leave the children with my mother and their paternal grandparents when I went to London, so the only change was that I was leaving sooner than expected.

On my last day at the Legal Resources Centre, two days after the stabbing incident, I went to a meeting at Bambayi in Inanda with senior attorney Peter Rutsch. The community was facing eviction from their homes and was in turmoil. At the meeting I met Lulu Gwagwa of the Built Environment Support Group. We were thrilled to discover that both of us were scheduled to leave for London to study for master's degrees and were booked on the same flight. She had previously spent six months in London and was more than willing to show me around.

Having just escaped a traumatic family drama and being thrown into the unknown, I was relieved to have someone who might provide support in an enormous, strange new city where I would be spending the next twelve months. I was due to start my fellowship within weeks, but I was leaving under emergency circumstances, with accommodation arranged at short notice through our extended family. My father had visited London and shared some of his experiences so I was eager to spend time there, but my excitement was tinged with uncertainty.

The Mqotsi family were waiting at Heathrow Airport to collect me, and they gave Lulu a ride to Euston Station. My new friend was staying with exiled author, poet and cultural activist Mandla Langa and his family. Lulu and I both arrived in London earlier than planned. She had become too 'hot' due to her political activities and was forced to flee South Africa. Like me, she had temporary accommodation until her room at a university residence became available. I got to know Mandla and his family and became a frequent dinner guest at their home. I met Mandla's older brother, Advocate Pius Langa SC, who became Chief Justice of South Africa. In the way of life, which allows wheels to turn slowly within each other until cycles complete in the most surprising ways, Bhut' Pius and his family had been our neighbours in D Section, KwaMashu, though I had had no connection with him at the time. We had lived mere metres apart but had to travel to the other side of the planet, to the United Kingdom, to meet there. We formed a beautiful friendship.

I was still in shock from the dramatic breakdown of my marriage and it was part of my healing process to immediately share my history with these new friends from home and away. The story rolled off my tongue, and very quickly almost everyone in the tight-knit South African community and others I met in the UK heard about my collapsed marriage. The telling finally liberated me.

I received a letter from Sheiks while I was in London, in November 1988. He wrote that he had been shocked to learn that I had left Durban prematurely. He asked that we try to patch things up and get back together so we could build a future for our children. It was a lengthy, five-page letter. My response was slightly mean. I wrote on the reverse side of the last page of his letter: 'Never, ever will that happen. This is the end of the road.' I put his letter in a new envelope and posted it back to him.

Towards the end of my time in London, I purchased a youth Eurorail ticket that allowed me to explore some of the continent by train without much expense. I set off on my European adventure as soon as I completed my exams, taking the ferry to Calais. My first train journey was to the university town of Marburg in Germany, where my high school friend Xoli was studying engineering. My inclination was to spend extended periods in a place, getting to know its people and their ways. Germany became my base, and I explored it thoroughly with Xoli and her friends. We travelled to Berlin, where we visited the Brandenburg Gate and saw the Berlin Wall in what was to be its final few months of existence – though no one knew it then. We spent several nights clubbing in the world-famous Berlin nightclubs. Meeting people in the South African exile community was a bitter experience. As I watched them feed off the energy of anyone with connections to home, my heart would break. In the detailed conversations about everything that was happening in South Africa, the arts were a very significant means of enlivening the connection to their roots.

I went to Switzerland next where I saw my friend Rauof Mazou who had studied with me at the London School of Economics and Political Science. We borrowed his parents' car and toured parts of Switzerland and France. Although Italy, Greece and Spain were beckoning, I was suddenly gripped by the most intense homesickness. After more than a year away from South Africa, my family and my children, I felt an existential confusion. What was I doing in Switzerland?

With two weeks remaining on my train ticket, I turned tail and headed back to London. I booked my flight, made a quick visit to Brixton to shop for gifts for friends and family and boarded a plane to South Africa. I had been away for fourteen months.

I returned in October 1989. Sheiks had met someone new, whom he wanted to marry. The divorce summons I had issued before I left South Africa had not been acted on and had to be reinstated. Sheiks got his divorce and that was the end of it.

Home

South Africa was the most exciting place to be in the late 1980s. The post-apartheid dispensation was under discussion and participating in think tanks imagining a new country was energising and challenging. People from all walks of life contributed their everything to the process. The meetings would usually start with an inspirational message delivered through a struggle song or poetry. The stories and perspectives of participants would reveal many intersecting and contradictory issues. How would a post-apartheid country soothe our disconnectedness after we had been pitted against each other – racially divided, poor and rich, differing political tendencies, women and men, young and old, differently educated, differing cultural sensibilities, vulnerabilities, levels of generosity, compassion and selflessness? How would we acknowledge and heal the common and differing stories of our personal and collective history? Would the new nation provide space for all of us to confront our participation in violence, racism, misogyny, bigotry, economic exploitation, climate change and environmental degradation? How would we nurture our growth towards connectedness, kindness, creativity and love?

The imagining, dreaming and creation of a post-apartheid South Africa was an opportunity for us all to encounter our humanness as we contributed to building a new society. Yet it was clear to me that our efforts would not provide sufficient space for all of us to learn our individual strengths and transcend them to build a new collective.

This attempt to build a new South Africa was captured in the Preamble of the Constitution of South Africa, which became the supreme law of the land on 4 February 1997 after President Mandela signed it into law:

> We, the people of South Africa,
> Recognise the injustices of our past;
> Honour those who suffered for justice and freedom in our land;
> Respect those who have worked to build and develop our country; and
> Believe that South Africa belongs to all who live in it, united in our diversity.
>
> We therefore, through our freely elected representatives, adopt this Constitution as the supreme law of the Republic so as to –
> Heal the divisions of the past and establish a society based on democratic values, social justice and fundamental human rights;
> Lay the foundations for a democratic and open society in which government is based on the will of the people and every citizen is equally protected by law;
> Improve the quality of life of all citizens and free the potential of each person; and
> Build a united and democratic South Africa able to take its rightful place as a sovereign state in the family of nations.
>
> May God protect our people.
> Nkosi Sikelel' iAfrika. Morena boloka setjhaba sa heso.
> God seën Suid-Afrika. God bless South Africa.
> Mudzimu fhatutshedza Afurika. Hosi katekisa Afrika.

THE POLITICAL VIOLENCE THAT HAD spread across the country in the late 1980s significantly escalated during the transition period from 1990 to 1994 and it was a prominent feature of the country's first national democratic elections in April 1994. The Human Rights Committee – a non-governmental organisation that monitored rights violations in South Africa – estimated the number of deaths related to political violence at 101 each month between July 1990 and August 1993. A horrific increase in deaths related to political violence was registered in July and August 1993 (605 in July and 705 in August, compared to 267 in June 1993). From 1990 to 1992 I lived with my mother in D Section, KwaMashu where I was actively involved in the establishment of African National Congress structures and its Women's League. Our political engagements were hijacked by violence, defending communities and peace-making. The sound of gunshots from home-made guns and automatic assault weapons were commonplace, particularly at night.

In 1992 I had the shocking realisation that I was becoming desensitised by the violence and deaths. I was accompanying a film crew shooting a documentary on the political violence for the BBC. I went with the crew to film activists at a hide-out on the outskirts of Ntuzuma north of KwaMashu as they performed rituals intended to protect themselves against attacks. We left the area in the early hours of the morning but rushed back around 5am after receiving news of violent skirmishes that resulted in several fatalities and homes burnt to the ground. I experienced no revolted bodily reaction to the sight of a charred human body in one of the burnt houses, and as I walked out I realised that I was shocked by what the violence had done to me. Why had I not looked away or thrown up when I saw those human remains? Was I that brutalised? How would South Africans recover from such levels of violence?

The civil war posed a significant threat to the peaceful transition. Post-apartheid talks without credible and effective peace structures made no sense. Addressing more than 100 000 people at an ANC rally in Durban on 25 February 1990, two weeks after his release from twenty-seven years of imprisonment, Nelson Mandela called on the people of Natal to put an end to the crushing violence, saying, 'My message is this: Take your guns, your knives, your pangas and throw them into the sea… Close down the death factories. End this war now!' His call was a significant talking point in communities, ANC structures and among young people in particular. It marked the beginning of serious efforts to build and activate structures and networks for peace.

I had attended Mandela's rally but the stadium was too packed for me to connect with him, even though hearing his voice moved me and that entire gathering. I saw him again in August 1990, during his visit to the University of Natal. It was an immense experience. He was a towering figure – physically, and in terms of his presence. With an audience projecting attention, love and admiration onto him, Mandela appeared to grow in stature before our eyes – becoming a superhuman. He reflected all our focused energy and seemed to glow with a halo of light. I could not take my eyes off Mandela. When he spoke, his words were imprinted in my heart. I succumbed to him like a fan of a movie star. Even as I talk about being captivated by Mandela's charisma, I am aware of the dangers of idealising any human being in this way. We may all need to apologise for negating Mandela's humanness through our idealised notions of who he was.

On the day of Mandela's visit I spotted an extremely handsome fellow in the jubilant crowd. Serendipity had it that he and his friends joined mine after the event. I invited them to my sister's flat that coming Saturday, for her birthday party. He showed up with a friend and, like us, they were still flushed with the euphoria of having seen Mandela, which made for the most amazing party. Bathed in Madiba magic, we laid the foundations for a relationship, and life was good.

Soon after my sister's party, while driving to KwaMashu, I had a serious car accident. I was driving at a reasonable speed as I took the offramp from the N3 onto the N2 towards Stanger. In no time at all the VW Golf was no longer moving forward but spinning around in uncontrollable circles, colliding with the highway railing. My only thought as time went into slow motion was that I should keep my eyes open so that I could bear witness to my death. Miraculously, I came out of the accident physically unscathed.

Nevertheless, I was unable to touch that car for months afterwards, relying on my mother and new boyfriend for lifts. When Christmas approached I sent the car for repairs. My boyfriend was going home for the festive season and I would have been stranded without transport. Even though I never spoke about it, I knew that I had been traumatised by the accident. But after the car was repaired I got back onto the road.

It was a major step to date again. In the UK, following the traumatising assault and spectacular collapse of my first marriage, I had one intimate relationship, which very quickly proved to be a big mistake. I decided that I was going to be free, living the way I chose for the rest of that year. After I had been back home for several months and found balance and stability, I opened myself up to dating again. My new relationship was exciting.

In the early 1990s my new boyfriend's work required him to leave KwaZulu-Natal for Johannesburg. I had considered South Africa's dynamic and exciting largest city too fast for my sanity. Jozi was at that time the centre of an emerging new South African culture. People of all races mingled freely in the newly liberated city, immigrants from other African countries made it their home. Kwaito, a new musical style, reflected those varied cultural influences. The heart of the new South Africa beat hardest in Johannesburg, an almost uncontrollable space where people created new lives and made dreams a reality, and where it was as easy to have all hopes crushed by crime, injustice or sheer bad luck. Generations of South Africans have faced moving to the Big City, it is part of our cultural mythology reflected in the Hugh Masekela jazz poem 'Stimela', the colonial-era movie *Jim Comes to Joburg* and the name of iconic Afro-pop act, Mafikizolo.

I was ready to make the move to Joburg. I had been putting off the process of getting legal practitioner qualifications and this presented an opportunity to do pupillage with the Johannesburg Society of Advocates to qualify as an advocate. My application was accepted in February 1992. Despite being the catalyst for my move, my boyfriend never relocated to Joburg and the relationship fizzled out. During my pupillage, I made a point of introducing myself to all the black advocates practising in Johannesburg and discovered that all of them were committed to supporting pupils, sharing notes that helped us take in the large volumes of material we had to sift through in preparation for the Bar exams.

My application for admission as an advocate was generously settled by Advocate Vincent Maleka SC and moved by Advocate Tsepo Sibeko SC. Advocate Julia Trim was my Master, and with her quiet demeanour got me a heavy schedule as I shadowed her in preparation for matters and court appearances. Women advocates regularly invited us to coffee or lunch where we debriefed on our experiences with pupillage. I had regular content sessions with Advocate Ishmael Semenya SC, who shared his practical methods of understanding the many workflows involved in legal practice. Advocate Legoae Pitje SC, whose tragic death breaks my heart to this day, gave me files to work on and discussed the drafts I submitted.

A month before the bar exams, I reduced my observation of court appearances. I was living in a flat in Hillbrow – in a block called Sunset Place, on the corner of Van Der Merwe and Klein Streets. For the first time in my life, I decided to smoke to relieve my stress. I bought myself four packets of Vogue Slims from a corner cafe. When I took a break from my studies, I sat on my windowsill with a glass of cold water and a long, slim cigarette. I imagined that I was watching the city lights in an exotic location elsewhere in the world, inhaled the smoke, took my mind off the books and relaxed. After I wrote the exams I had two unopened packets of cigarettes, and never smoked again.

The results came out in July. I had achieved the necessary standards and I was an advocate. I started pupillage rather late in March 1992 and sat the Bar exams in June, but passed first time because of the practising advocates who generously cared for and supported the pupils.

When I began practising I realised that being admitted to

the Bar was no guarantee of success. Life was hard. Most of the matters I handled were assigned pro deo. I was appointed by the state in criminal cases to represent the accused. It was difficult to break into the legal mainstream as I was not from Johannesburg and had not done the networking necessary to secure briefs.

In May 1992 I started a relationship with an advocate practising in Durban. Three months later, in the early stages of my career as an advocate, I fell pregnant for the third time. At the end of February 1993 I packed my bags and headed back to my mother's home in Durban.

The two unopened boxes of cigarettes were still among my belongings, and resurfaced at the most inopportune time. One night my sister Jackie overheard my mother muttering to herself, 'Yhooo, even Louisa is smoking now... My house is really going to burn down!' Jackie had been smoking since her first year at university and was convinced that my mother was completely unaware of her vice. But my mother's use of the word 'even' spoke volumes.

In April 1993, when my third baby Themba was about two weeks old, I set up chambers in Salmon Grove to begin practising as an advocate. It was incredibly difficult to build a practice while looking after a baby. Again, I managed to eke out a living from criminal pro deo matters and cases handed to me by other advocates. My child's father was also an advocate and would pass work on to me whenever he could. He was well established in the criminal law area and a mighty player on the social scene.

Themba was a small baby, born at St Augustine's Hospital and weighing 2.5kg. He was nicknamed Baby Chicken. His delivery was quick and almost painless. He arrived before expected and brought joy to our family. My body felt renewed after delivering Themba, as it had done after his brothers were born.

My mother moved out of KwaMashu. Her sleep was regularly disturbed by intruders setting off the house alarm system. She bought a firearm and trained to use it, without telling us. One night after the alarm system was triggered more than once, she fired shots into the air as a warning to the intruders. A bullet ricocheted off a surface and went through the kitchen window of Sis' Beauty and Bhut' Pius Langa's home across the street. Fortunately, no one was injured. Our mother reported that the Langas were very gentle with her the next morning when they came to establish what had happened. She bought a flat in Berea and I lived with her for a few months before renting a place in the same building. I had a good support system, raising Sheikani, Rikhado and Themba with my mother in close proximity. But she began a new phase of her life, qualifying as an estate agent.

'For me, life didn't begin at 40. It begins at 60,' she told me. 'So, if you're going to keep on having babies, don't plan on me looking after them!'

I had no quibbles with that. She was absolutely right.

I was struggling, my practice wasn't getting off the ground. I attended a conference in Johannesburg where I learned that the Centre for Criminal Justice (CCJ) at the University of Natal in Pietermaritzburg was seeking a researcher. I immediately applied and was offered the position.

In November 1993 I moved to Pietermaritzburg with my children and began work at the CCJ. We examined the transformation of the police services, how communities participated in their own safety and security and shifts in human rights relating to the criminal justice system. We conducted workshops and published the outcomes of our research in preparation for the transition to a democratic dispensation, already underway.

After three months at the CCJ, I accepted an offer to join the Natal Provincial Interim Transitional Task Team under the leadership of Bheka Shezi, a practising attorney in Durban. Its task was to prepare for the establishment of new governance structures after the elections. Some blueprints were generated during the political negotiations at the Convention for a Democratic South Africa and the task team studied how existing bureaucracies operated at municipal, provincial and national levels, proposed how to build relations between existing and emerging systems and designed new systems aligned with agreed constitutional principles and democratic values.

While doing this work I saw, for the first time, a jostling for power and the purchase of patronage. Every political party had the right to participate in meetings discussing the transition to democracy. However, for some people, bribery was their only approach to power. We were invited to the homes of politicians or expensive restaurants to be wined and dined. Even after we consistently declined their offers representatives of certain political parties kept plying us with gifts. I found it slimy and repulsive. This was a deeply entrenched culture, it was the way power replicated itself and how things were done. In this parallel system of achieving political objectives, people expected you would bend and break the rules meant to safeguard the best interests of all, in exchange for personal favours.

Before I had time to settle into the Provincial Interim Transitional Task Team processes, I was invited to apply for a role at the Constitutional Assembly. South Africa's democratic elections were guided by an Interim Constitution. The Constitutional Assembly was tasked with drawing up the country's binding new constitution, complying with agreed principles written into the Interim Constitution. One of the key tasks of the assembly was organising nationwide public participation programmes to solicit the views and suggestions from the people of South Africa on their new vision for the country.

I applied, was invited to interview and appointed as one of two deputy directors for the Constitutional Assembly. It was a quick process, and I was required in Cape Town to begin work almost immediately.

I uprooted my children again, after a mere nine months in Pietermaritzburg. When we arrived in Cape Town in August 1994 and checked into the Woodstock Garden Court hotel, we met Abdullah Ibrahim and Sathima Bea Benjamin in the lobby. We chatted and Sathima gave me a cassette tape of her music. She was a beautiful jazz singer. I was almost speechless when Abdullah invited me to his performance that evening with the Cape Philharmonic Orchestra at the Nico Malan Opera House. He offered me two tickets. I was delighted to attend the historic disentanglement of a symphonic orchestra from whiteness in South Africa. My heart was already open to orchestral and classical music, so this shift brought warmth to my heart.

I invited my brother Bheki Zondo who practised medicine in Khayelitsha to join me at the concert and he gladly did so. I had met Bheki during my LLB studies at the University of Natal while he was a medical student. We immediately related as brother and sister, allowing the fact that we are not biological relations to remain in the realm of minor detail. The concert was a commemoration of the tricentenary of the arrival of Shaykh Yūsuf of Macassar in South Africa. Victor Ntoni, a highly fêted musician, conducted the orchestra and the concert featured the accomplished jazz musicians Basil Coetzee, Ezra Ngcukana and Vusi Khumalo. Their performance brought me to tears of pure joy. It was a beautiful and memorable introduction to Cape Town.

My Sathima cassette tape became part of my treasured musical collection that was stolen in an armed attack at my home in 1998. My stolen musical treasures included a collection of Cabo Verdean popular traditional music known as morna that had been given to me by several people in Portugal in 1997. I love this music that vividly strings together the intricate story of the people of the West African island nation. Morna stirred me into the rhythm of the rumba and the merengue without a care about my lack of expertise. I don't understand Creole or Portuguese but the music whispered to me the laments of slavery, forced migration, drought, epidemics, poverty and the erasure of the dignity and humanity of people of Cabo Verde. It edified the spirit of resistance, embraced the rupture of love and spoke of deep longing for a beloved homeland. My collection included the music of Cesaria Evora (Queen of Morna), Adriano 'Bana' Goncalves (King of Morna), Mayra Andrade, Tito Paris and other more contemporary artists.

Our first home in Cape Town was in Bantry Bay, on the city's Western Seaboard. Rikhado and Sheikani went to the nearby Camps Bay Primary School. The boys were active and mischievous. They used the money I gave them for taxi fare from school to buy sweets and snacks, then walked the three kilometres home. Sheikani was eleven years old at the time and Rikhado was seven. Rikhado's reckless, independent spirit could not be dampened down. Marion Sparg, who had been deputy director at the Constitutional Assembly, shared on her Facebook page a memory of Rikhado that illustrated this perfectly. She answered the phone in my office on one of our late nights at work in the mid-1990s.

'Hello? Can I speak to Louisa Zondo please?' asked a young voice on the other end of the line.

'Louisa is not in at the moment. Who is speaking? Perhaps I can help you...'

'It's Rikhado. Can you please tell me how to cook fish fingers? I'm at home and I'm hungry. I want to have fish fingers, but I don't know how to make them.'

'Um, I don't think it's a good idea for you to try and cook them right now. Your mommy will be home soon, and I'm sure she will bring you some take-aways, so please just wait for her.'

Rikhado was always challenging himself. Ready to venture into the unknown. Even if it was only for fish fingers.

My mother joined us in Cape Town in October 1994, two months after our arrival, and launched the next phase of her career as an award-winning estate agent. Our family had relocated, and I had begun my new role. Perhaps my most important one yet.

The Constitution: Honouring the experience of life

On election day in April 1994 I was in Pietermaritzburg where I was working at the KwaZulu-Natal Provincial Transitional Task Team. I wanted to experience as much as possible of the day's events so I spent the morning at home, absorbing as much as I could of the news from across the country. I had constant goosebumps. Something amazing was going to happen to all of us. I joined a queue at midday, sharing the euphoria of the people slowly making their way to the polling station. The three hours I queued flew by, it meant nothing that I was on my feet that length of time. My body was carried by the joy of the experience. It was a journey into hope.

A few months later I became engaged in shaping the Constitution of the new country we had voted into existence. When I joined the Constitutional Assembly we had eighteen months to finalise the constitution-making process. I had not envisaged how intense this would be, although I was aware of the political negotiations that had brought us to this point, I had not been involved in the day-to-day work of bringing the parties together.

I knew I was going to be involved in a historic moment and I was up for that. I knew that the work would be hard because of the extremely tight deadlines. What I hadn't imagined was that the process – in particular, the public engagements – was going to require a huge amount of effort, love, commitment and enjoyment.

Hassen Ebrahim was the executive director of the Constitutional Assembly and Marion Sparg and I were deputy executive directors. The team had been pulled together quickly, so getting us to gel was a huge task. Everyone needed to understand the work required without much induction and orientation. We had to get on with it. Hassen had the ability to carry the lightest of hearts in the most intense situations. All you had to do was give him a cigarette, and he would keep the mood focused, light and enthusiastic.

It was a positive environment, and many of us became attuned to the spirit of being open and collaborative. There was no room for fights; if conflict arose it had to be dealt with immediately before we all moved on. Our meetings were well structured and we focused on setting priorities. We would report back where necessary. There were no meetings that allowed people to show off as important, relevant or successful. Our meetings were an opportunity to align and realign, request and offer support and maintain a healthy overview of the entire organism as we each fulfilled our tasks.

I was responsible for overseeing the legal and research areas of work, media and media liaison, public participation and education programmes. The constitution-making process was supported by a panel of independent experts who refined the draft text that emerged from the political negotiations without substantively amending politically settled agreements, while adhering to the principles in the 1993 Interim Constitution

We found new ways to invite, receive and provide input and feedback on the process, and we were deliberate about introducing more effective and user-friendly ways of communicating. This included the use of plain language, and communicating with images and animation where possible when sharing information about our work. The Constitutional Assembly called on everyone across the country to recognise that drafting a new Constitution was important as it would shape their lives and offered them the chance to have their say. Groups of politicians travelled the length and breadth of the country to consult with communities on behalf of the Assembly. Thousands of written submissions were received, recorded and analysed by a team that decided which theme it related to and brought them to the attention of the relevant theme committees.

South Africans made a huge investment in the public participation process. The Constitutional Assembly teams went into communities to raise awareness about human rights and stimulate discussions about the meaning of a Bill of Rights. They educated people around the country on the responsibilities of local, provincial and national government, and the division of powers in a constitutional state.

The logistics of getting politicians to the most remote areas across the country to ensure they included citizens' participation in drafting a new Constitution required an enormous amount of attention to detail. The South African Communications Services (SACS), a state communication agency that bore the legacy of the apartheid state, worked with us to plan the logistics for reaching the areas where these engagements were held. Our travelling groups would sometimes encounter difficulties in reaching their next public engagement. SACS officials had access to networks that could solve all our problems.

In no time, an aircraft would be commissioned to fly to a remote area and take the team to another equally remote area, where they would be accommodated in surprisingly comfortable lodgings. There would be evidence, such as a shooting range, revealing that the lodges had been used for military-related activity. It left me fearing whether the new South Africa would ever achieve the level of integration of all the systems the country needed. I worried whether we were taking stock of all state assets so we could manage them effectively.

The vibrant community consultations were critically important. If the people involved in the constitution-making process failed to understand the aspirations of all citizens, the Constitution would not take root in their hearts and in the way they lived as South Africans. Appropriate connections had to be established between how people in their various circumstances experienced life, and how the Constitution sought to honour their experience.

At a public engagement focused on religious, linguistic and cultural rights, women asked how the Constitution would deal with ukuthwala, the practice of men abducting a girl or a young woman to compel her family to agree to her marriage. In the past the cultural practice had assumed some consent from the woman Today ukuthwala has become a means of abuse, a violation of women's human rights. Men abduct women and minor children who are not their lovers or fiancées and keep them hostage, exposing them to many forms of exploitation, including rape and slavery. Men often get away with this crime under the guise of exercising their cultural practices. How the Constitution would deal with ukuthwala was a question begging to be asked.

Engagements like these helped me understand how continued discussion about the Constitution could help us review what changes were required to our traditional and cultural practices, and how such change could emerge in caring and sustainable ways. Discussions about a Constitution presents an excellent opportunity to raise awareness about the basic principles of human rights law and constitutional law. The question whether the human rights in the South African Bill of Rights are absolute rights often fascinated participants at our community engagements. After people become aware that the rights provided for in the Bill of Rights may be limited by law of general application if it is reasonable and justifiable in an open and democratic society based on human dignity, equality and freedom, they often question the implications of limitations on rights that they believe are of a higher order than others. Quite often, people expected that the right to life would be absolute.

The constitution-making process was led by the chairperson of the Constitutional Assembly Cyril Ramaphosa. His deputies were Roelf Meyer and Leon Wessels. Their management committee was made up of representatives from the political parties, and a larger group of people attended the plenary meetings. The leadership of the assembly had to negotiate the entire text of the Constitution and find resolution on prickly matters. The secretariat was responsible for recording these processes, and the accuracy of the record in a political negotiation such as this could make or break the process. We had to ensure that the assembly's records didn't become another site of struggle because of perceived misrepresentation of what transpired in engagements between political parties.

I learned a lot about techniques of moving people from their positions. Listening deeply and empathetically was a thread that ran through all decision-making relating to contentious issues. Sometimes tempers got in the way of politicians representing parties that stood in opposition to each other. When politicians allowed themselves to engage while valuing each other, resolutions to intractable problems emerged. With empathetic listening, resolutions were freely proposed, very often preceded by the phrase: 'If it might be of assistance to Honourable XXX...' At other times engagements would be characterised by the constant butting of heads and a refusal to listen to other viewpoints, which made it hard to arrive at solutions.

There were as many views as the political parties in the room and more. Even within political parties approaches weren't necessarily in sync, so being able to synthesize different views, to try to understand where they were coming from and to suggest a possible resolution were lessons I picked up at the Constitutional Assembly. Ramaphosa was a master of reducing the distance between views and supporting everyone to resolve their differences. I gained respect for Wessels, because he would do all of that with humility and light-heartedness.

The deadline to produce a new Constitution could not be breached, and a culture developed in the assembly of doing what needed to be done for as long as it took until it was completed.

I have a photo of me with my head on the desk as a deadline approached that expresses this work culture perfectly.

I was particularly invested in the Bill of Rights. I had my fourth son, Ntobeko, while working at the Constitutional Assembly. His middle name is Bill for two reasons – after the Bill of Rights and because my father's name was Bill. The most important guide to drafting the Bill of Rights was the achievement of human dignity, and the clauses on discrimination set the country on the path to making that outcome possible for all. We were going to ensure that discrimination was elaborately and comprehensively prohibited, and I knew that the Constitution would really transform our country if used effectively.

I did not get much sleep the night before the Constitution was adopted. We entered the National Assembly and took our seats in the officials' section. We could see the excitement in the spirits of the politicians. They seemed to be in sync. The speech delivered by Deputy President Thabo Mbeki, titled 'I Am an African', elevated me in the way no political speech had done before. It moved me in all sorts of ways – in my sense of being and my spirituality. I began to cry. I was crying for Louisa who had forgotten that she was part of creation and contributed to all of creation. Mbeki called on us to remember that we are not only the material instruments of life. We are everything; we are connected to the mountains, the seas and the air. We are connected to each other, no matter where we come from, how we look, what we think. We are each other. That was big for me.

The constitution-making process was a legacy for our country that we had a duty to keep alive. Over the decades since it was adopted we lost touch with the principles and spirit of our constitution, and the mutual respect and consensus that gave birth to it. We can do things differently today if we again speak and teach about our true, fundamental way of being as a people, captured by our Constitution.

Key to this will be getting young people to become invested in the Constitution, to evoke its power while exercising their rights and working towards their dreams. I am a mother of four sons. I have worked with young people in higher education, and experienced the trauma and the soul-crushing disappointment of trying to fit in, to make sense of a system that alienates you in so many ways. When we were young we were often silenced while trying to find our relevance, our space, acknowledgement of our dignity and our abilities despite our shortcomings and limited capabilities. We encountered violence as we tried to contribute to the shaping of humanity and we resisted.

We need to create an environment that listens to young people and seeks to collectively create a future. That starts with understanding the present and how it merges with the past. Older people attending this intergenerational dialogue should approach it with humility. This will open space for the younger ones to engage. Young people don't understand the Constitution, they don't trust it and they don't see the liberation that would be rooted in its implementation. There is redress for their battles in the Constitution; it is a tool they can use to achieve their liberation.

As older people, our view shouldn't be that we've done it and we know it. We should understand what's causing the mental illness and imbalance among us right now; what's causing our inability to relate to situations, and our responses born from frustration. We must understand what's causing the violence and hostility we have towards each other so we can start working towards a common future.

The adoption of the Constitution was pretty much my last day on the job at the assembly. I had been interviewed for a role at the new South African Human Rights Commission, which was established in terms of the new Constitution to support constitutional democracy and human rights. A week after the adoption of the Constitution I was in Johannesburg working with the commissioners to set up the new structure. I didn't attend the signing of the Constitution, but I celebrated in different parts of the country, travelling to schools with the Human Rights Commission to mark its entry into law.

The constitution-making process succeeded in creating a guiding document that is relevant to people's lives. I cannot claim that it brought the Constitution into people's hearts, but it made it relevant to people's lives. We could have continued to build on that strong base by creating more avenues for engagement. One of our national weaknesses is that after we establish an institution, we seem to believe that it will take the process further and we can hand over everything. For the Human Rights Commission, with its mandate to promote respect, protect and advance human rights, that duty almost always seems to rest on the institution. It does not have sufficient resources to build a culture of awareness of human rights. What we need is a country that engages with human rights across the board and works to build a human rights culture everywhere.

The Constitution frames how I step into all sorts of relationships – in the organisations where I work, how I relate to people and how we tackle the issues that arise when we engage. It is drawn into all my interactions because it has become a framework from which I can talk to anybody about how I assess what's happening. For many people the Constitution has no relevance or it is seen as an impediment to progress. People often mistakenly say the Constitution prohibits us from dealing with crime. It is an incredibly limiting perspective to argue that because the Constitution outlaws the death penalty, the police and society are incapable of dealing with crime.

The Constitution has been called the soul of our nation, its conscience. It also has a practical role, providing pillars that ground us and allow us to navigate any set of circumstances. It provides a framework for ongoing change. Sadly, we seem to have abandoned it and left the Constitution to fend for itself. That is a shame, because it means we cannot reap the benefits of the powerful document, the supreme law of our land. After fighting for freedom, we never fought for the Constitution that enshrined those freedoms, we took it for granted.

After the ratification of the Constitution, the Truth and Reconciliation Commission (TRC) facilitated a cathartic process and a belief that we were over the worst and could now move into a new, nirvana-like state. The TRC acknowledged that there were gaps within its frame of reference. It was not tasked with examining the economic effects of apartheid, focusing only on the political calamity. The TRC's recommendations touched on the need for rebuilding communities, healing, meaningful reparations, monuments and creating spaces for people's stories to be told in connected communities. Those proposals were completely ignored by the government. From time to time over the years since the TRC submitted its final report to the government it has been mentioned in passing, but the need for real, practical healing has never been addressed.

Many people believe that the TRC process was a betrayal because it did not touch their lives. It brought no change and their suffering is still so real. The pain remains. The mysteries about the disappearance of their loved ones remain unsolved. We are doing nothing to rebuild, to heal the hurts. History is still with us. The political is personal and the personal pain that scars the lives of so many of families in our country has not been healed. It is still so real.

Cape Town blessings

I had no regrets about putting a distance between myself and Themba's father when I moved to Cape Town. I could not sustain that relationship. When I had worked and lived in Pietermaritzburg it was still too close to his home in Durban for my liking. During our first few months living in Cape Town I savoured the arrival of spring and enjoyed the city warming up as Christmas approached. My mother had also moved to Cape Town and many friends came to visit, blessing us with their energy, and confirming that we were in the right place at that stage of our lives – and our new country's rebirth. Our first Christmas season in the Cape was an amazing period.

There was a law conference in Somerset West, about 50km outside Cape Town, in January 1995 which Themba's father attended. We met up one evening and I offered to take him to a party with some of my Constitutional Assembly colleagues. We had a good time and I drove him back to his hotel after we left the party. I was exhausted and reluctant to make the stressful, slightly dangerous hour-long drive back to Bantry Bay in the middle of the night. I agreed to spend the night in his room but insisted that my boundaries remain in place. They did not and the next morning I rushed to a chemist for the morning-after pill. I swallowed a second dose twelve hours later but the medication had no effect.

This pregnancy took a heavy toll. We moved, with my mother, to Lansdowne, which was closer to her estate agency practice in Mitchells Plain. I told no one about my pregnancy, but the changes in my body were obvious. My face changed and I developed large acne sores. I could not confide in anyone. Then one day my mother sat me down, said she could see I was no longer my normal happy self and asked what was happening.

I broke down and told her that I was pregnant again and I did not know how I would cope. My mother calmed me down and said we would handle it together. We would raise the child in the same way as Sheikani, Rikhado and Themba. The first step my mother took to welcome her new grandchild was buying me maternity clothing.

I began preparing for the birth. I was five months pregnant and had not yet sought prenatal care. I consulted a gynaecologist and expressed my desire for a baby girl – three boys were enough. But I was informed I would again be blessed with a boy. As my confinement drew near, I decided to name my child Ntobeko, which can be expressed as humility in English. Although I had at first regarded my pregnancy as a setback, I now appreciated that it was a blessing I would humbly accept.

I arrived at the hospital in the late morning after I began feeling unwell following a few busy hours at the office. I was an old hand at giving birth, so my gynae arrived at the delivery ward to find me casually browsing through a magazine, despite having contractions.

'You're looking quite relaxed,' he joked. 'We'll see in a couple of hours whether you're still looking so smug!' Two hours later he returned to check on me and not much had changed. I was biding my time, keeping myself occupied until the baby came.

'How are you still like this?' he wanted to know.

'This is my fourth baby,' I replied. 'I know how this process goes.'

It was a painful birth but at least I was familiar with the pain.

I knew what it does, how long it lasts and that it would eventually pass. I was relaxed until my baby arrived; there was no need for drama.

There was one problem that I had not anticipated. When I brought Ntobeko home from the hospital, Themba, who was two years and seven months old, found it extremely difficult to accept his new brother. During visits at the hospital Themba had been curious to meet the new baby but he wasn't ready for him to come live in his home. He pulled at Ntobeko while he was suckling, as though he resented any care and attention I gave the baby.

I had never heard of sibling jealousy and subsequently learned that it can be quite common, that it is an aspect of human psychology. Knowing that did not make it any easier to deal with. Themba was physically interfering when I nursed and interrupting my attempts to take care of Ntobeko's needs. I asked my mother whether we should send Themba to his father in Durban to ease his troubles. My mother was very clear that this was not a good idea. 'Themba feels like you are giving Ntobeko more attention than him,' she said. 'He is worried that you are going to replace him. Rather speak to Themba and give him attention while the baby is around so that he can see you love him and care for him even though we have another child.'

She explained that sending Themba to Durban might confirm to him that he was being replaced by the new baby. If we did that, we would be inflicting on him the very harm that he was trying to protect himself from – being separated from his mother. I explained to Themba that he was loved, that I loved all my boys equally but, because he was new, Ntobeko needed my attention. After some time Themba found his ease.

At the time of Ntobeko's birth in October 1995, we were nearing the end of the eighteen-month constitution-writing process and working at a hyper-energetic level. The frenetic deadline to draft a new Constitution meant that I was back at work at the Constitutional Assembly full-time within a week of Ntobeko's birth. Mentally, I was able to compartmentalise mothering by working, but my body did not recover as quickly as it did after my other sons were born. I was healthy but my body did not return to its previous thirty-two waist size dimensions, for about six months.

Soon after returning to work I joined my colleagues for a Saturday hike up Table Mountain. We planned to go up in the cable car but the cableway was closed due to bad weather. We decided to walk up the mountain. I knew it wouldn't be easy to hike up to 1 084m above sea level, but I was excited by the prospect. I carried thirteen-day-old Ntobeko in a child carrier strapped to my front and two-year-old Themba on my back. My mother came with to help care for the boys. The wind was howling at gale force, and we were dressed for a casual lunch. Unwisely, we began walking up the mountain.

About halfway up I realised the folly of our decision and turned back. Our group had disbanded and we were all walking separately. My mother, sixty-five years old at the time, was wearing sandals entirely unsuited to mountain climbing; she fell behind soon after we started our attempt to reach the summit. After several hours on the mountain I eventually staggered back into the parking area at the cableway. I was exhausted but safe. There was no sign of my mother. The mountain is a maze of paths and when I didn't catch up with her on my way down I hoped she had taken another route and would be waiting for us at the bottom.

We waited for two hours for my mother to arrive in the parking lot. When it started getting dark we began panicking. We alerted the emergency services and the Mountain Club. More time elapsed before they arrived and it was pitch dark when the search began. Just as the rescue team set off my mother came walking down the mountain, barefoot, clutching her sandals and looking extremely unhappy. Although her body was wracked with pain she was a remarkably resilient woman. After a long, hot bath and a day's rest, she was back in action. These are the trials and tribulations of living in Cape Town. We embraced the experience and it remains one of the happiest times of my life.

Love and the cataclysm

My lovely baby Ntobeko had to be weaned off the breast after a few months. My Constitutional Assembly responsibilities were coming to an end and a new way to serve was opening up. In March 1996 I was offered employment at the newly established South African Human Rights Commission (SAHRC) as its first CEO, to lead the team which would get this crucial institution up and running. The commission was established by the Constitution, as one of the Chapter Nine institutions intended to protect South Africa's constitutional democracy. Other Chapter Nine institutions include the Public Protector, the Commission for the Promotion and Protection of the Rights of Cultural, Religious and Linguistic Communities, the Commission for Gender Equality, the Auditor-General and the Independent Electoral Commission.

To prepare for my new role I travelled to Cameroon with SAHRC Chairperson Dr Barney Pityana, Deputy Chairperson Shirley Mabusela and the Public Protector Advocate Selby Baqwa. We attended a conference of African national human rights institutions that explored the establishment of an African network and setting standards for national human rights institutions. I had to take malaria tablets to travel to Cameroon and this meant I had to stop breastfeeding. I felt extremely sad for Ntobeko and myself. My other children breastfed for two years or more and he was on formula from about five months.

I left my family in Cape Town while I moved to Joburg to find premises and interview prospective employees for the commission. We began work at offices in downtown Johannesburg and later moved to premises at the Isle of Houghton office park in Parktown where we remained for many years.

Through my work at the South African Human Rights Commission I reconnected with Kumi Naidoo, head of the South African National NGO Coalition (SANGOCO). We had first met in London in 1988 while I was studying at the London School of Economics and Political Science and he was studying at Oxford University. He had come to London for a seminar hosted by Shula Marks at the School of Oriental and African Studies. Born in Cape Town, Shula is now emeritus professor of history at SOAS.

A South African academic, whose name I cannot remember, had been invited to present her reflections on the state of the country. South Africans in the UK made a point of attending such gatherings to ensure that flawed perspectives did not go unchallenged. The speaker earned herself a flurry of hard questions when she stated that apartheid legislation did not violate human rights but only curtailed human rights. This was met with relentless challenges from the audience. She was quizzed about her awareness of the systemic gross violations of human rights entrenched in apartheid and whether she knew apartheid was a crime against humanity, and very quickly lost all composure. With a quivering voice, she stuck to her assertion that South Africa only curtailed human rights to the extent that it was necessary.

The South African students who had attended the seminar gathered afterwards at the student union for drinks. A lanky young man with a head and face full of hair caught my attention. He was filled with energy and his hands flew all over the place when he spoke and laughed. Something about him stirred my heart and everything in me. I felt that ridiculous skip of the heart and that flow through my body — I think it's a stream of joy.

We didn't talk much, and I don't think Kumi registered anything about me. Fate was on my side though, because a new structure of South African students in the UK was soon launched. Kumi and I attended the launch weekend where I spoke to him and exchanged contact details. I called his college house in Oxford during the Easter break and discovered he was spending the holidays with his girlfriend at her family home. Over time the image of those expressive hands faded.

Like me, Kumi is from Durban. He is from Chatsworth, a historically Indian township established in the 1950s. When we returned from the UK — Kumi in 1990 and I in 1989 — we almost crossed paths doing ANC work. We were both organising in our communities, contributing to rebuilding the ANC in the country after it was unbanned. An essential part of this work involved connecting people who had been segregated for decades by apartheid. In 1991 the Chatsworth Interim ANC Committee, through Kumi, invited me in my capacity as the secretary of the KwaMashu ANC branch to address a community meeting in Chatsworth. I was invited to tell the story of myself, the journey life had taken me on and what I made of it at that point in the South African transition.

Kumi has kept a copy of a pamphlet inviting people to the meeting. I could not get from KwaMashu to Chatsworth that day. I did not have a car of my own and my mother's old yellow Datsun station-wagon had gone for repairs and had not returned on schedule. I had no way of reaching anyone by phone after office hours, so I simply did not pitch at Kumi's meeting. Almost five years passed without any contact.

After I was appointed at the SAHRC I contacted Kumi to talk about how we could build a culture of human rights and map pathways to expanding and deepening human rights education. I thought a collaboration with SANGOCO would be mutually beneficial and impactful. Kumi loves to tell the story differently. He likes to suggest that I secured an appointment with him because of my interest in him. His version of the story is that when we met for breakfast we spoke about many things but he has no recollection of any discussion focused on work. He does concede that he sent an email afterwards recording the discussion and actions we planned to pursue.

One of the new public holidays proclaimed by South Africa's democratic dispensation was Human Rights Day on March 21, commemorating the day of the Sharpeville massacre when apartheid policemen shot and killed sixty-nine residents of Sharpeville and Langa who were protesting against the racist pass laws. For Human Rights Day in 1997 the SAHRC organised a conference. Kumi was invited to address the gathering and facilitate some of the sessions. This marks our transition from being comrades to becoming friends. We played squash on the courts at his flat in Yeoville. We went out for what we termed 'getting to know you' dinners. They achieved their desired effect, we got to know each other very well indeed. We became regular visitors at each other's homes.

In June, six months after our breakfast, Parliament invited me to speak in Cape Town about the public participation process in the making of the new Constitution. Kumi was also in the Western Cape at the time, attending a meeting in Franschhoek of the board of Alliance Capital, an asset management company in which SANGOCO had secured shares. He called to find out how my day had been and raved about his hotel room. I drove to Franschhoek to see the beautiful room that had so impressed Kumi. My bearings are poor so it took me two-and-a-half hours to navigate a journey that usually takes an hour from Cape Town.

When I arrived in Franschhoek it was obvious that I was not going back that night. The question in the morning was, 'Will you be coming back?'

The answer was, 'Yes, of course.'

When we returned to Johannesburg we privately called ourselves friends with a cherry on the top. The friendship evolved into a relationship where we became partners. Our organisations worked with others to organise a National Men's March Against

Gender-Based Violence on 22 November 1997, under the banner 'Real Men Do Not Abuse Women and Children'. The march was a collaboration between SANGOCO, the Human Rights Commission and the Commission on Gender Equality. This effort accelerated the passing of the Domestic Violence Act the following year.

SANGOCO and the Human Rights Commission also collaborated on the National Poverty Hearings, an inquiry into the effects of apartheid on the social and economic wellbeing of those who had experienced its worst impacts. Panels of eminent members of society including SAHRC commissioners, listened as people gathered in their community spaces to tell what connections they experienced between apartheid and poverty. The socio-economic impacts of apartheid fell outside of the mandate of the Truth and Reconciliation Commission and attempts by civil society to have its mandate expanded to include focus on apartheid's impoverishment of black people failed. Our hearings considered people's proposals on breaking the cycles of poverty. We launched the report in Soweto before the second democratic election, partly as an appeal to all parties to intensify their efforts at addressing poverty and inequality.

Kumi and I were making plans to move in together. He had already brought some of his clothing to my house and his sister, who was studying dentistry, would remain in his Yeoville flat. My friends suspected that I was involved with someone, so I organised a small birthday dinner for the big reveal. Kumi cooked an amazing spread of curries, and we had a beautiful evening at my home in the Johannesburg suburb of Kew. My friends were thrilled to meet this person who was clearly making me feel happy and fulfilled. They welcomed him warmly, he was happy to meet them and everyone got on like a house on fire. The party continued until late into the night and at some point Kumi went to sleep, strategically providing an opportunity for my friends to offer their honest critique of him and us.

It was the early hours of the morning when I said goodbye to the last of my departing friends. I locked the house and did some basic cleaning before joining Kumi as he slept peacefully in bed. Around 2am I woke up to the sound of strange men in our bedroom, and our lives were never again the same.

They were shouting and at first I could not figure out what was happening. My mind began recounting my steps before coming to bed. Did I lock the sliding door from the braai area to the kitchen? Did I lock the front door? With my heart pounding as I lay on my stomach, I remembered I had locked everything. So why were people in our bedroom? What do they want? What are they saying? I decided not to move, not to make a sound, to keep my eyes shut.

My body was shaking. I buried my face deeper into the pillow as I tried even harder to keep my body still. I closed my eyes tighter when they hit Kumi. I didn't know what they were hitting him with but I could hear the blows landing. I know they tied him up because I heard Kumi complaining that it was too tight. He was beaten again when he asked them to loosen his bonds. One of the men came to my side of the bed. He pulled my arm and I was on the floor.

I kept my eyes shut. I heard the sound of feet shuffling on the coir carpeting. It sounded as though the men were walking in slippers. I realised someone was speaking to me: 'Namhlanje, hayi kuphelile ngawe! Hayi siyakukhawada namhlanje.' (Today is the end of you. We defeat you today.) My body could not stop shaking. I was dragged down the steps in the passageway into the lounge. I kept disappearing into sleep. When they asked me to write down the combination code for a padlock securing the gate, I wrote it on the piece of paper they put in front of me.

I heard the sound of a car engine outside and listened as it faded into the distance. I fell asleep again. It was quiet when I opened my eyes. I spotted a knife, grabbed it and clutched it tight. I was furious, I wanted to kill the men. Where were they? I fell asleep again. I woke up with the knife in my hand and the realisation that Kumi was in the bedroom. I cut the ropes that bound him, put on a housedress and ran out of the front door, urging Kumi to hurry. My heart was pounding, I was afraid they would come back.

I headed for the BP petrol station on Corlett Drive. Kumi was struggling as I urged him to walk faster because they had tied him so tight it had affected the circulation to his legs. The distance from our house to the garage was only 850m but I was struggling to breathe when we got there and Kumi was in no better state. The employees at the petrol station let us use their phone and I called Jackie, told her what happened and urged her to come quickly.

It was around 6am when we got to the BP. Jackie lived in Lonehill some 23km away, and we estimated that it would take about thirty minutes for her to reach us. The wait was unbearable. I could not bear standing inside the petrol station's shop, I was suffocating. Standing outside in the open did not feel safe. Jackie came and it was such a relief. She had told my friends what had happened after they left the party, so when she drove us home they began arriving.

Their presence was relief beyond expression, I began to feel as though I had been restored to safety and good order. My energy returned. The feeling took me back to the day before we buried our father. Teachers brought school friends to visit us and all I wanted to do was play with them. I spoke too fast and was hyperactive as we played a game of touch in our backyard and I never wanted it to stop.

I found the 'what happened' questions very difficult to answer. I had terrible pain on my elbow but no clue how I received that injury. The side of my face looked bluish from bruising but I had no idea how that had happened. Kumi told me later that I had been beaten and pulled off the bed before I was dragged to the front room. He thought my elbow was hurt when I was dragged down the two steps into the lounge. He said one of the intruders had thrown a bed sheet over me because I was naked. He told me that when they rummaged through the closet they found my advocate's robe and asked what it was, and I responded that it was my graduation gown. He was surprised that I could not remember that when I was asked what degree I had graduated with my response was social work.

On reflection I have allowed myself to imagine and went on to hold as truth that in those moments of uttermost fear, desperation and helplessness my father was there with me. He had a social work degree. Had I said I was a lawyer the likelihood was that our lives would not have been spared. I remain deeply grateful for that protection.

As we made plans for the next steps that Saturday morning after the attack I battled to bring myself together, it was impossible. I had been scattered into a million pieces and I didn't know where to start gathering it together again. Kumi said I called my boss Barney Pityana, chairperson of the SAHRC, to tell him that I wouldn't be coming to work on Monday. I was so disconnected from reality, Kumi said, that I smiled when I told Barney that we were fine. The truth was that as I was speaking on the phone I felt as though I was dying. Smiling and pretending that everything was fine felt like salvation from that death. That became my pattern.

I did not know how to explain this destabilisation to myself, let alone anyone else. I was constantly afraid, empty, lost and filled with hateful anger. I went for two trauma counselling sessions at the Centre for the Study of Violence and Reconciliation that made me feel suffocated. I could not bear the compression. Kumi hoped that in due time I would be able to start counselling again, so he let me be. He continued the sessions for several months. I was afraid of everything, disconnected from everything and filled with hate and furious rage for everything all of the time.

Journalist Sharon Chetty was among the friends who came to the house after the attack. She could not resist commenting on the fact that the suitcase Kumi had brought from his flat had been chucked outside my gate and his clothing was strewn on the grass. 'Kumi, I have long been telling you about your dress sense,' she said. 'Now you have to do something about it. It is so bad that even the lumpen proletariat will not accept your clothes.' We laughed deep and hearty because Kumi was not known as a snappy dresser. My laughter was practice for my pretence that I could carry on even as I was breaking apart.

Jackie took me to see a doctor at the Sunninghill Hospital. Years later she told me she had been hoping a good doctor she knew would be on duty and was delighted when he was. I walked out of the consultation a few short minutes later, spitting with anger as I headed for the exit berating the doctor for asking stupid questions. We had agreed that I would stay with Jackie and draw comfort from her. But she said that after a few hours I impatiently asked her to take me to Kumi in Yeoville. I was restless and remained so for a long time.

My mother arrived in Johannesburg two days after the home invasion. She had relocated to Portugal with my oldest sister Tandi who had been assigned to a diplomatic post in Lisbon. I went to Jackie's home where my mother was staying and I spent time with her. When I spoke to people about the attack I immediately got a terrible headache. My mother did not interrogate me, aside from asking if they had hurt me. With tears flowing uncontrollably I showed her my hurt elbow and the bruise healing under my tears.

I never returned to trauma counselling even though Kumi kept begging me to go. I had flashbacks of the attacks that were triggered in my sleep when I sensed Kumi entering our bedroom. He told me my body would spasm and my face would be contorted with fear during the flashbacks. During some of them I fell off the bed onto the floor. At times I responded to Kumi as if he was one of the attackers. I knew that Kumi was going through a hard time but I could not bear talking to him about the attack. Sometimes, in company, I put on a happy, easy-going attitude and we would joke about how the police got certain things wrong in the statement when we reported a case of housebreaking, assault, robbery and the theft of household goods, laptops and my car.

The police officers who attended to us at the house wrote down the statement, so we had to go through a dreadfully slow and painful process of narrating what had happened. Kumi said that when the attackers realised that I was an African woman, they asked aggressively and repeatedly, 'where's the bitch?' At first he was confused by the question but realised that they assumed that his wife was Indian and they needed to manage the risk of her returning to the house. He told the intruders that I was his wife and it was my house.

A few days after filing the complaint, we went to the police station and read the statement that we were expected to sign. It had some mistakes but the one that really stood out was where it said the assailant asked us where the 'beach' was! When the police told us that the fingerprints were inconclusive, it was clear to us that pursuing our case would be futile – and that became another wound inflicted. Replacing things that were lost in the attack was immensely difficult. I broke down and cried in anger several times as I tried to get a new identity document, driver's licence and bank cards.

In June, on the urging of his doctor, Kumi bought tickets for a seven-day holiday in the Comores. It was idyllic and peaceful. We went on excursions around the main island and enjoyed great food and fantastic dance music every night. Jackie collected us from the airport when we returned. When we were alone I confided to her that although the holiday had been great, I could not bring myself to touch Kumi, not once.

It must have been devastating for Kumi to try to understand why I wouldn't talk about the attack and what it meant for us when I constantly refused to seek counselling. Not talking to him about the assault meant that I gave him no support as he dealt with his sense of helplessness about his inability to protect me. I can only imagine how sad and isolated he must have felt. He was going through almost unbearable trauma. He was also unable to touch me in any way.

In the chaotic aftermath of the attack I did not pay attention to my menstruation cycle and realised at the end of March that I had not had a period for two months. I took a pregnancy test and it came back positive. Kumi and I managed to be gentle with each other as we discussed the result. We used protection all the time but remembered we once suspected leakage. I was certain that I was in no state to have a baby and told Kumi that we had to have an abortion. We investigated the Mary Stopes services and within a week I secured an appointment for the procedure.

Until now, I have never spoken about this to anyone except Kumi. He was pained by the long absences of his daughter Naomi, who lived in the UK. She was the centre of his life. He had been keen to proceed with the pregnancy but only articulated this in later years. As time passed, we allowed ourselves brief moments to talk with sadness about how old our baby would have been and imagined what she or he would have been like.

A few months after my world had been torn down to its foundations a new opportunity arose. I went to Portugal in 1997 and travelled from there to visit my friend Raouf Mazou in Switzerland. While I was in Geneva I went to the South African embassy hoping to speak to the ambassador Jackie Selebi, about opportunities at international organisations. He was out of town but I was invited to leave a note and my CV for him. Selebi got in touch and arranged a meeting when he returned to South Africa. He said there were United Nations organisations interested in South African representation. One of them was a new organisation, the Comprehensive Nuclear-Test-Ban Treaty Organisation Preparatory Commission established after the United Nations General Assembly adopted the Comprehensive Nuclear-Test-Ban Treaty.

The organisation's mandate was to establish a global monitoring system to prevent nuclear testing, giving effect to the treaty. I submitted an application for a position at the secretariat of the organisation with support from the South African Department of Foreign Affairs. I flew to Vienna for an interview and was offered the position in August of 1998.

Sheikani and Rikhado were living primarily with their father in Johannesburg. Sheikani was fifteen years old, enjoying high school life with friends and revelling in becoming a young man. When I introduced the idea of us moving to Vienna where I would be taking up a three-year assignment, Sheikani said he would visit me there, that he couldn't leave his friends and life in South Africa.

He was eventually persuaded to move to Vienna when his father fell into dire financial straits and had to downsize his life. My two younger boys had been living with their father in Durban from December the previous year when the care giver who looked after them absconded with bags of clothes. They arrived in

Johannesburg a few weeks before I was due to leave. My sister released my mother from Portugal so that she could live with us and support me with the children in Vienna. The family was back together again. Kumi remained back in South Africa and started looking for jobs that would bring him closer to us and to Naomi in Oxford.

Family values

Our time in Vienna was a landmark period for my children's growth. They were exposed to a new environment that allowed them to expand their life experience and mature rapidly. They blossomed at the international school they attended where there was a rich diversity of cultures, and they developed tight friendships with children from all around the world. Themba grew in leaps and bounds at the preschool he attended that exposed him to the world.

I took German lessons but made little progress. At the Vienna International Centre where I worked English was spoken, so I had little opportunity or need to practise my German. My schedule was busy, so I quit my classes. Yet three-year-old Ntobeko and five-year-old Themba picked up German with ease. My children could fluently communicate with locals in the Austrian-German dialect.

Sheikani, who had been reluctant to leave his South African friends, soon made a new set of buddies in Vienna. He had been a chubby little boy but when he turned sixteen he burnt off his puppy fat, began growing into his adolescent body and gained confidence. I was fearful as children are essentially given the keys to their adult freedom when they turn sixteen in Vienna. It's not unusual to see sixteen-year-olds consuming alcoholic drinks in public spaces and they seemed to be allowed to stay out till all hours.

Although the boys were attending international schools and I was working in an international environment I was aware that there are racist elements in many European countries, Austria included. When Sheikani and Rikhado stayed out late I was unable to sleep until I heard the door opening, signalling their return. I constantly feared that Sheikani might not ignore the taunts of racist skinheads he encountered and would respond. I doubt such risks occurred to him when he was out and about enjoying his freedom in an environment he considered absolutely safe compared to Johannesburg, so I suffered in silence.

Rikhado was on the cusp of adolescence at the age of twelve and idolised his older brother who was blossoming into a cool teenager. Instead of embracing him, Sheikani evicted him from their shared room for being smelly and untidy. Rikhado moved in with his grandmother. I saw how sad this made him but I felt unable to intervene. I learned how much Rikhado admired his brother when I bought new clothing for him once, a cardigan and a collared shirt that he rushed to try on. I caught him standing before a tall mirror in our entrance hall, admiring himself as he adjusted the collar and cuffs of his new shirt, muttering to himself, 'Now I look like Sheikani.'

Rikhado was going through the normal stages of pre-teen development. He might have had body odour and had not yet begun to use anti-perspirant or fragrance. This became the pretext for Sheikani to push him away and Rikhado struggled with that rejection for many years. Sheikani and I discussed this years later. He acknowledged that he distanced himself from his brother but he said he did it to protect Rikhado. He was experimenting with adult life and did not want Rikhado exposed to it. He couldn't have known at the time that this would leave deep scars on Rikhado.

I decided not to extend my three-year stay in Vienna after meeting the then deputy minister of minerals and energy, Susan

Shabangu, who represented South Africa at an International Atomic Energy Agency meeting. I had no idea who she was when I first set eyes on her but recognised a fellow South African by her dress. She wore a bright-orange outfit at an austere multilateral meeting, and so I went to ask if she was from down south. We began chatting after she confirmed that she was from Mzansi and I explained what I was doing in Vienna. She was surprised and told me I was needed at home. South Africa's nuclear agencies had recently been restructured and needed expertise.

I began the transition back to South Africa by enrolling the children in South African schools while I completed my tenure in Vienna. Rikhado returned to Brynevan in Bryanston, Johannesburg to finish primary school and his father enrolled him at Hilton College, the prestigious boarding school in KwaZulu-Natal, for high school. I fielded many calls from him expressing disbelief at his new environment. 'This place is just hard,' he said. 'Why are these people like this?' He declined my offer to move him to another school, saying he needed to stick it out and make his mark as a person who could survive those hardships. He eventually overcame the challenges of boarding school.

Sheikani had it more tough than his brother. He was in his final year of school in Vienna and we could not find a compatible school in South Africa. At first we thought he could study remotely at the Vienna International School but this was not practical. He completed his last year of school at the American School in Johannesburg. My mother returned from Vienna with the children, and she and my sister supported them while I completed my contract.

In September 2000, I began my new role as CEO of the National Nuclear Regulator. It manages the regulation of all nuclear facilities in the country, except for those in the healthcare sector. It was a new institution, brought into existence through legislation grounded in the vision of transforming South Africa's nuclear sector. Because of our history, South Africa had a dearth of nuclear experts. We urgently needed to build capacity, because even though we chose an anti-nuclear national strategy, we still needed nuclear physicists, chemists, engineers and all sorts of expertise to ensure we could regulate the environment effectively. Capacity-building was a major transformation focus of the regulator when I was recruited into its leadership, resulting in a National Nuclear Skills Audit being completed and the establishment of Women in Nuclear South Africa, to stimulate equitable women's participation in the field.

A major issue of that time, in the early 2000s, was the proposed Pebble Bed Modular Reactor, a public-private partnership comprising the South African government, nuclear industry players and utilities. When a country embarks on a major nuclear project such as that, no interest is served by the nuclear regulator not having an abundance of expertise required for effective regulation. The project had been funded by the South African government for many years, and was geared to establishing a small, gas-cooled nuclear reactor to meet some of South Africa's energy needs. It also attracted a great deal of environmental opposition.

The issues were complex and nuanced, and required careful analysis. From an economic perspective, nuclear power is not worth it. It takes an average of 14.5 years to bring a nuclear power plant on stream from the planning stage to operation. In the early 2000s, the wisest course of action for South Africa would have been to make the best use of the energy sources developed over many decades, while strategically introducing a new trajectory towards renewable energy in line with our own capacities and needs, while making sure that we were not hoodwinked by lobby groups and purveyors of technologies that might not serve our needs.

I worked at the nuclear regulator while Rikhado completed his schooling at Hilton and Sheikani went to study in Cape Town. Rikhado planned to take a gap year after he finished school in 2005 so that he could find himself. He wanted to live with his father in Venda and hoped to reconnect and strengthen their relationship. Unfortunately, Sheiks passed away in January 2006.

Sheikani was devastated by his father's death and was unable to finish his degree. I became conscious for the first time of how the stoic, emotionless façade I had built around myself was affecting my children. They looked to me for emotional cues and saw nothing. 'I'm struggling with my father's death,' Sheikani told me, 'I don't know how to continue. Everything is gone for me. And I've never once seen my mother cry.'

He saw me going about my life despite everything and asked himself why he was not able to follow suit. His relationship with Rikhado began to suffer. After the passing of their father all the tension that had built up over years about who belongs, who leads and who must follow, exploded. One day, in the depth of their grief, they began physically wrestling with each other.

'But he's my father too,' Rikhado said, crying.

'But you are not responsible. You are doing strange things,' Sheikani responded.

In hindsight, this should have been my first intimation that something was wrong with Rikhado, that perhaps he was dabbling in drugs. I pieced this together much later, but Sheikani knew more than me. It must have been terrible to watch his younger brother's anguish. He did not have the emotional connection to steer Rikhado in a different direction. But who knows what could have possibly steered Rikhado onto another path. The heartache of being unable to provide guidance and leadership when a younger brother most needs it must be hard to bear – after they lost their father Rikhado was especially vulnerable.

We were living in Epsom Downs in the north of Johannesburg. Rikhado had taken over Sheikani's room at the back of the house after his older brother had moved into an apartment. We were all living in Johannesburg, but I was watching my boys fall apart. Sheiks was still living in Venda when he fell ill. He came to Johannesburg for treatment and I went to visit him once with the boys at Helen Joseph Hospital. That was towards the end of December 2005 – only a few weeks before he passed. I left for India with Kumi to visit a yogic science and naturopathic centre in Bangalore, which was recommended by friends in India after Kumi suffered another bout of bad burnout from a year of incessant work pressure and travel in the roles of Secretary

General of CIVICUS and volunteer chair of the Global Call to Action Against Poverty. We were booked for ten days to cleanse, recalibrate and live healthily. We received news that Sheiks had passed on our sixth day at the retreat and I immediately made arrangements to return, but urged Kumi to continue with the programme.

I had expected that, after the funeral, the boys would return to their lives. But they were completely derailed. Sheikani returned to university but dropped out because he could not cope. Rikhado's plans for a gap year had been ruined. He enrolled for a degree in communications at Varsity College, which proved to be a terrible idea. Nothing he was taught made sense, nor did it relate to his aspirations. His grandma drove him to college every day, making a huge impression on his friends. She was a constant source of love and stability. Rikhado stuck it out but at the end of the year he asked if he could quit. He asked me to accompany him to the African Film and Drama Academy (AFDA) in Melville, Johannesburg. We collected information about the school and he said its programme resonated with him. He enrolled and thrived immediately. It seemed he had found his path.

He moved into a flat in Melville during his first year at AFDA. He settled into an independent adult life and Kumi and I would visit to drop off groceries. Then after a few months, we were worried to notice that he didn't seem to be eating the food we provided; he had lost a lot of weight. From being an almost thick-set sportsman at high school, he was skinny, so I increased my food deliveries to no avail.

In the third year of Rikhado's studies he lost an expensive camera that belonged to one of his classmates. He told me he had arranged with his friend to pay back the cost of the camera over a few months. He asked for my help with the payments and I agreed to assist. A few months later his friend called me and said Rikhado had not paid him a cent.

I confronted Rikhado and he admitted that he had not paid his friend, at first excusing his behaviour by claiming he had other bills to pay. After he was unable to tell me which other bills he had, I asked the obvious question: whether he was on drugs. 'Yes,' he replied.

It was a Saturday. I was visiting my sister Jackie at the Life Fourways Hospital, where she had been rushed with abdominal pains. I had this conversation with my son while standing in the small garden area outside the main entrance to the hospital. I went down onto my haunches when I heard my son's truth on the phone. "Since when?" I asked.

"I've been trying to stop,' Rikhado said. 'It's been a long time. I've been trying to stop…'

The barrier between us was torn down and I began speaking freely with him. I said he would never be able to stop on his own, he needed help. As I began to talk about treating his addiction I sensed a desire on his part to retract his confession.

'Everybody's doing it,' he said. 'I've been trying to stop, but everybody's doing it. Even when I went to Zimbabwe with Kumi, I was trying to stop.'. He had travelled with Kumi a few months earlier on a risky mission to film a documentary on atrocities in Zimbabwe, human rights violations and the government's inability to provide basic services. 'I've been trying to stop, but it's hard.'

'Okay,' I said. 'I'm coming home. Don't go anywhere. We'll talk about it when I get home.'

I called my minister, Reverend Mzwandile Molo, who I knew had more experience in dealing with such matters than I did. As I spoke to him it felt as though I had been stripped naked. He acknowledged how devastated I was about the news of Rikhado's illness and told me there was one thing I would have to remember: 'There is only one thing that your son is looking for; the only thing that is going to lead him through this, if he is going to pull through it at all. He is looking to see in your eyes that you love him. That's all he needs. He is looking to see in your eyes that you have not rejected him. Because right now, he believes he is not deserving of love. He feels like he is nothing. I know it will be hard. You are disappointed, you are in shock. But just remember that he will look into your eyes, and he is looking for love.'

I entered the hospital to visit my sister. I didn't mention

the news I had just received and was relieved to learn that her condition was not serious. My mind was whirling and my knees wanted to buckle but I managed to keep it together until I reached home.

Rikhado confessed that he had long ago dropped out of college after he was unable to perform. I told him it was okay; we would work things out together. He confirmed that he wanted to stop doing drugs and started making calls. I contacted every friend and colleague who might have had leads on rehabilitation service providers. I scoured the internet. Information came pouring in. There were facilities in Oaklands, Kempton Park and Randburg, all of them regarded excellent.

I went to church the next day. I had arranged to meet my minister after the service. When I sat down with Reverend Molo everything poured out. We prayed together, which gave me strength and I felt strong enough to face the next step in the marathon journey I was about to undertake with my son. As I left the church, I met one of my Secret Pals who had been at Inanda Seminary. Thandeka Mgojo was accompanied by her husband Mxolisi. I blurted out that I had just discovered that Rikhado was using drugs and my tears poured out. I was blessed to have a friend of so many years to comfort me at that moment of extreme fear and confusion.

During that disastrous time when I tried to imagine what my son was going through I cried until I felt like I was a tiny pebble. I felt I had no other option but to give myself over to a higher power. I was depleted. I had an image of myself as a tiny, smooth stone lying on the bed of a stream. I began to surrender to the flow of the universe. At that moment of surrender, I felt lifted. I realised that the outcome of this problem was probably not in my hands. I had no previous experience of addiction but I could surrender, and walk the journey with my son.

Every rehab centre I discovered required Rikhado to be clean before he could be admitted. That was our first objective and I decided that I would not let him out of my sight. On the day before our appointment at Houghton House, the rehabilitation centre we had chosen, he tried to escape my constant presence by claiming he had errands to run. I refused to let him out of my sight. 'You and me, right through. Until we go in tomorrow,' I told him. He was grumpy all day, I could see he was struggling.

The next day I didn't go to work. I took him to his consultation with the admitting social worker at Houghton House. Rikhado arrived with a positive spirit but his mood changed when it was decided that he would be admitted as an in-patient and be assessed over two weeks. He tried to claim that he had important things to do, but this was something that the social worker had heard before. She was able to convince him to commit to the two-week assessment.

Rikhado's two weeks extended to six months, followed by a further three months at a halfway house. He went through all the stages of recovery and was determined to heal. But in the creative spaces where he was beginning to make his mark, it was unsafe for an addict in recovery. He had relapses several times after he returned to his social circle and as he began to establish himself on the music scene. But he was equally determined to make it as a music artist and literally played with fire.

Rikhado was making music and writing lyrics. Growing up, music had not been a big focus, although it was a huge part of our family life. My sisters and I built up a good collection of vinyl when we were teenagers. A former neighbour told me years later that he enjoyed lingering outside the Zondo house where there was always good music playing.

We had named Rikhado after Ricardo Groenewald who sang the 1980s hit song 'I Love You Daddy'. It became a self-fulfilling prophecy because he loved his father beyond words. My son's stage name was Riky Rick and his album *Family Values* is my favourite gift from him because Rikhado gave his whole self to us in this work. I have asked my family to play the track 'Home' on repeat when I die. I love 'Mthande' because it lifted me up when my November 2019 lupus diagnosis sent my world into a vicious spin. Rikhado used to call just to sing the chorus of the song 'Egoli' by Mlindo the Vocalist featuring Sjava to me. The song continues to have a special place in my heart.

We hadn't known that Rikhado had the voice to carry a tune or that he loved music until he reached his teens. At the age of fourteen, while he was goofing around with his cousins, he broke into song and everybody stopped what they were doing to listen to his beautiful voice. During a trip to the US he acquired a beat machine. It looked like a useless square machine with white buttons to me, but I subsequently learned that it was a Roland SP 555 sampler. He used it to write and produce many of the songs that would help him break into the hip-hop world as a rapper and a producer.

He networked diligently in the hip-hop community. He entered rap battles in Braamfontein, went to hip hop shows and open mic events. Despite his short stint at the African Film and Drama Academy, filmmaking was also a focus. It contributed to his success as an artist, all his music productions were accompanied by a video, a cover image and the clothing he would wear. He was always a fun, exciting person to watch, whatever he was doing. He established a video and photography company with a friend and they purchased professional equipment. He was constantly involved in photography and videography. He expressed this dichotomy in some of his songs where he raps about being behind the camera when all he wants to do is make music. Eventually he chose music as a career. But throughout his journey he battled addiction.

In 2013 Rikhado met Bianca Naidoo who became his manager, business partner, wife, mother of his children and the constant light in his life. Meeting Bianca changed his life. He had finally found someone who felt like home. Bianca's daughter Jordan was about to turn five when they met and Rikhado was captivated by both of them.

After releasing several singles, Riky Rick had his first big hit with 'Amantombazane', first released in November 2013 and followed by an award-winning remix in June 2014. He began winning awards for his music and videos, launched clothing lines and a music festival. He was celebrated and revered in South African popular culture. I maintained my role of the mother who looked out for him and helped when it was needed. I made sure he always knew that he could ask me for anything.

In 2012 he met artists from the USA and hoped to work with them. I helped him move to Los Angeles, where he lived for almost half a year. He hadn't been sober when he arrived in the States and became really depressed. The US artists were unimpressed by his music, they found it too similar to their sounds. Rikhado did not make it in the States but the experience led him to develop a sound that was more distinctively South African, that resonated more strongly with audiences across the country and beyond. He worked hard on his music when he lived in Amsterdam with Kumi when Kumi was the executive director of Greenpeace International. Rikhado connected with artists from the African diaspora who were living in the Netherlands. He began to see how his music could combine elements of English, isiZulu and other African languages. He refined this over the years into a distinctive style that felt authentic and found a wide audience.

Rikhado was fluent in isiZulu and English after growing up in KwaMashu and being raised by Zulu women. Yet he yearned for his Venda heritage. He seldom spent long periods of time with his father. In the track 'Papa's Song' on the *Family Values* album, Rikhado lamented the absence of his father in his life, said he missed him after his death and expressed the pain of his absence during his childhood. In loving kindness and with a reconciliatory tone he said that his loved ones never cared about his possessions, they only needed to experience his presence. There always seemed to be too much going on in his father's life to make lasting connections with his sons.

In a YouTube interview with Loot Love, titled 'Riky Rick Speaks on Being a Nomad, Building His Character & His Venda Side', my son discussed how he held the paradoxes of a pattern in his life where he always seemed to be in places where he was not expected, such as being a descendant of Venda royalty who was not able to speak TshiVenda. He said he held all the paradoxes with respect. He shared his pain and yearning for deeper connection to his father and about losing the sense of stability and belonging in his life because I constantly moved cities.

In the same interview Rikhado said there had been many blessings and losses throughout his life. He had framed his engagement with life on the basis that nothing lasted forever but he appreciated the gifts that came with constant movement. Watching that interview, I realised that Rikhado had attended six primary schools in five cities on two continents. How I wish I had a deeper awareness of what a young person might lose in such a transient life and allowed an opportunity for all my children to discuss it. There were benefits but there was also an underlying, unspoken restlessness associated with the fear of impermanence. Perhaps, if I had been less closed off and had been more present with my children, I might have seen what so much change might do to them and done something about it. Although I no longer have a chance for redress with Rikhado, I hope for second chances with Sheikani, Themba, Ntobeko and all my grandchildren.

That constant movement and changes of circumstance gave Rikhado the ability to relate to people and make friends quickly, to fit in quickly and easily in different environments. 'You will find me in places that you don't expect to find me,' he used to say. 'My passport will have many stamps.'

While KwaMashu remains my idea of home, that feeling was not as well developed for Rikhado. When he was in Hilton, home was Johannesburg. After living in Durban, home was Cape Town. He would say, 'I was born in KwaMashu, I grew up in KwaMashu, home is Johannesburg.' Heritage was a difficult issue for Rikhado. He loved his grandmother on his father's side. She is a vibrant spirit who is alive and well, and ninety-four years old at the time of writing. He would often drive from Johannesburg to Polokwane to be with her. He looked a lot like his father and grandmother and felt settled in their space.

As he built a family with Bianca, Rikhado battled with depressive episodes. Bianca would call and ask me to come when he was in a bad state. I would not fully understand what was going on, but I would spend time with Rikhado, who would hardly talk. He seldom shared his deepest feelings but on the few occasions he confided in Bianca, she told me what troubled him. She said his pain came from feeling disconnected from his family. He complained to her that when he was a teenager, I would often come home from work, and lock myself in my room and not want him there.

Rikhado asked me often to tell him the story of my life. I kept promising that we would talk about everything but we never found an opportunity. It would probably have been an uncomfortable, but much-needed discussion. In November 2021, after another call from Bianca for my help with Rikhado's depressive moods, I promised to write the story of my life in letters to him.. He said he would like that. But I couldn't share my story with my son. It seemed that I was unable to speak or write my story. At that time, I did not know what the reason was, but now I know that I handled the many traumatic experiences in my life by avoiding them and my mind helped me by shutting them out. It was a form of protection from the devastating truth of my past.

Nothing else to offer

Bianca called me in February 2022, her words strangled by the sobs she was suppressing. 'Something is wrong,' she said. She had gone to Rikhado's studio to check on him after dropping off the children at school and found it locked. His car was outside. 'I can't get in,' she said, 'I've found a note in the car. Please come, Mama. I'm scared.'

'I'm on my way B,' I responded while I negotiated with myself to keep breathing and begged my heart to slow down. I was in a conference room at the LaWiida Lodge where a three-day Oxfam South Africa strategy session was about to start. As I made arrangements for transport from Tshwane to Rikhado's studio in Barbeque Downs, Midrand some 28km away, Bianca and I continued our conversation on WhatsApp messages:

07:45. Me: 'The Lord is with you and all of us, all the time, B'
07:55. Bianca: 'Mum I'm scared'
07:55. Me: 'Just call on his name! Just call on Jesus'

I WAS DESPERATE, willing my heart to stay in its place, my head to stop spinning, the air not to feel so thick as it entered my nostrils and my rubbery legs to work. Within ten minutes Sibusiso Zulu was driving me through thick rush-hour traffic. I called Sheikani, explained what Bianca reported and asked him to urgently check on the situation. I sent a WhatsApp to Bianca to say I was on my way and asked how she was holding up.

Sheikani called to say Rikhado's friend Bheki Nkentshane had managed to pry the studio key out from under the gap at the bottom of the door and unlocked it. He and the Major League DJ twins Bandile and Banele Mbere found Rikhado hanging from a rafter and cut him down. A bellowing noise sent me rolling on the back seat of the car. I cried out from the depths of me: 'My son has died! Oh God, my son has died!' All the energy flowed out of my body as each breath turned into a sob. I gathered myself and realised the rest of the family had to be informed. His maternal aunt Makhadzi Denga Makhado was overseer of all family matters. After calling and greeting her, I established that she was home and asked if she was seated. After she told me she was in bed I delivered the news. The notification of a call from Bianca interrupted my explanations so I apologised and disappeared on my son's aunt. Bianca told me Bandile, Banele and Bheki were rushing Rikhado to the hospital, that I should meet them at Waterfall City Hospital. I called Makhadzi again to tell her there was hope.

My heart was filled with expectation as we arrived at the hospital and walked towards the entrance. When I reached the lobby, Sheikani called. 'Hayi, he didn't make it, Ma. Rikhado is gone.' I went down, prostrate on the ground. Every ounce of energy exited my body. I heard people scurrying about and calling for a wheelchair. Hands pressed down on my right arm and back and a voice called to God Almighty, Lord of Mercy and Jesus. Sibusiso, who drove me to the hospital, witnessed my despair turn to hope, then turn to despair. He prayed energy back into my body and helped me off the floor. Hospital employees offered me a wheelchair but I pointed to the emergency department about 100m away and told them there were children waiting there who needed me on my feet so I could be there for them. I called on Jesus for strength with every step I took towards my people. Banele, Bandile, Bheki and other young people were in the emergency department. I gathered them in my arms but found I couldn't utter a word. I asked to be taken to Rikhado and was led to the resuscitation room.

My son was lying on a steel bed, dressed in a white CottonFest tracksuit. A male hospital employee was removing cables attached to his body. He looked like himself. He was still my son. His expression was slightly forlorn because his lips were parted, but it looked as though he was lying quietly on the bed. As I drew closer to him a loud cry erupted from me. I ran my hands over his entire body, first his right side then his left. I cupped his head and prayed for him, for Bianca, Jordan, Maik and all of us. I prayed for God's mercy and love to hold us up.

I noticed that his right palm was completely open while his left one was slightly clenched. I sensed that his open hand reflected that he had given everything he could and had nothing else to offer. The slightly clenched hand said he was unable to take care of some things and relied on us to do so. The wellbeing of his children was the most urgent need. I was calm when I left the room. It was 23 February 2022 and my second-born son had died from suicide.

Themba arrived and I held him tight for a long time before taking him into the resuscitation room and giving him a moment alone with his big brother. Sheikani came, got his long hugs and joined his brother. Ntobeko was the last of my sons to arrive and seeing him so deflated just broke my heart. Bianca's body quivered as I approached her. I held her tight and told her that I had seen Rikhado and prayed with him. I told her that he looked peaceful and beautiful. I asked her to come into the room and see him, I promised I would be with her. She was unsure and I could see how impossible this moment was for her. We entered the resuscitation room and Bianca stood in the doorway crying. After she gathered herself and went to the bed, I left her to have a private moment with her husband.

I had to call Kumi in Berlin. 'Oh God, how am I going to do this? Please Lord, give me the strength,' I prayed as I dialled his number. I greeted him gently. He sounded tired. I asked if he was home, and he confirmed that he was. I asked him to get a glass of water and sit down in a comfortable place, I had news. When he confirmed that he was seated I told him that Rikhado had hung himself at the studio and had died. Listening to him break apart was unbearable.

'I'm so sorry, babes, I'm so sorry Kumi,' I told him. We cried together for a few minutes. I asked him to tell Naomi and his siblings Kovin and Karmini before they heard about it on social media.

My next call was to my best friend Xoli. I could not tell my sisters this news over the phone. Xoli undertook to go to Centurion, where both my sisters lived, to break the news.

The hospital staff told us that the police had been notified and they would come to take statements and complete other procedures related to death from unnatural causes. A family counsellor was on her way. The police had not yet arrived by noon and we were worried Jordan and Maik would hear about their father's death. My Secret Pals had received the news and they were frantic. As I walked towards Bianca's friend's car in the hospital parking lot, I heard loud screams. The Secret Pals had arrived.

They rushed towards me and we embraced. Surrounded by their love and support my heart literally broke. The pain in my chest was immense. I tried to find relief through deep breaths, but the agony would not abate. Massaging my chest area brought no relief.

We were summoned from the parking lot before we could leave. The police had arrived and we were required for their procedures. After a slow process of taking statements, we confirmed that Rikhado had left a note for Bianca and the children but refused to give it to them. I was given access to the hospital photocopier and made a single copy of the note. I gave the original to Bianca. I wanted to ensure that we controlled access to the note so we could monitor where leaks to the media originated. It was leaked, and we have no doubt who was responsible.

Sheikani undertook to stay at the hospital to wait for the morgue services to take Rikhado for an autopsy, necessary for the issuing of a death certificate. We were finally free to go home and break the news to the children. Bheki had collected Jordan and Maik from school and brought them home. We found them on the couch facing the TV. Hugging them and drawing them into her tiny body, Bianca said she had bad or sad news. Very early that morning Rikhado had passed away. Jordan crushed everything inside me when she cried out, 'Why? He didn't do anything wrong!'

She had the same pained response in 2014 when she was five years old and Bubbles, a beautiful black cross between the Fox Terrier and the German Shepherd breeds, had to leave before her brother Maik's birth. I was worried that a big dog living in their house might not be healthy. Rikhado took Jordan with him when he dropped Bubbles at the SPCA, hoping she would understand that this was the dog's new home. The cages were jails, Jordan decided, and it wasn't fair that Bubbles was going to jail for no good reason.

Jordan and Maik cried in their mother's arms for ten long minutes. Bianca told them that it was going to be very hard for them – and all of us – to deal with Rikhado's death. She promised that she was available to talk whenever they needed her. It was okay to feel sad, all of us were feeling very sad. Rikhado left beautiful messages for his family and Bianca read them aloud to her children.

I expected the children to be immobilised by grief and incapable of finding joy. But that afternoon Maik had the company of a friend, and they played in their usual way. He went to his mother a few times, though, and told her he missed his Dada. Jordan was a quiet and thoughtful teenager who spent a lot of time in her room. Friends came to visit and that was comforting, restoring some of her normal vibrancy.

A few weeks after Rikhado's death the children started consultations with a child psychologist who gave them tools to express themselves, understand their emotions and regulate them. I kept the scrap paper Maik and his cousin Mia used to write and draw tributes to Rikhado, who was Mia's godfather. I thought back to my eight- and nine-year-old self, and wondered whether at that age I understood the notion of Rest In Peace. They understood it.

It became a house rule at Bianca's home that everyone had the right to their feelings – they were allowed to feel anything, whether sad, confused, angry, joyful or afraid. In the first few days after Rikhado's passing Maik needed to speak to his father and Bianca proposed they use the many photos of Rikhado scattered all over the house to greet and talk to him. That ritual was only required for a few days. Rikhado's children remembered him and his quirks. From time to time we would hear them comment, 'Hmm, you know what that was right? That was Dada!'

They missed him but they know he lives in them through the love they have for each other. On 4 February 2023 CottonFest, the music festival Rikhado initiated with friends to showcase freedom in fashion, art, culture and music, took place in Johannesburg. Jordan attended wearing a pair of jeans that had belonged to Rikhado. I found that gesture so precious I hugged her and would not let her go. Bianca said she kept a good amount of Rikhado's clothes and belongings for the children. It warms my heart to see the children thrive. I often think about Rikhado's slightly clenched left hand, and I ask what am I called to be for the children. Perhaps just the comfort of a gogo.

In the days following Rikhado's death our family received outpourings of love and generosity from friends, his business partners and associates, fans and people who had been touched by his life and death. People were deeply struck by grief. My expression to the many people who came to Bianca's home as I hugged them was a genuine 'I am so sorry'. I felt their sadness in palpable ways. Rikhado's life created a huge family for us, and we were connected by grief.

The Secret Pals were a huge support. They organised a roster for the daily provision of delicious food, catering for the large numbers of people who came to the house. A prayer service was held every evening, seamlessly organised by teams that attended to everything including the live streaming of the services. Xoli strung many parts together. She had not gone home since the day Rikhado died, staying with me at Bianca's home and taking care of everything. Kumi's friends and relatives came too and supported us with much love and care when we needed it most.

The chest pain that started at the hospital on 23 February got worse. After evening prayers the next day, the constriction in my chest was unbearable. I asked Kumi, who had arrived from Berlin, to take me for a check-up at the Waterfall City Hospital. After several tests, a doctor confirmed that my heart had no medical issues. She gave me a muscle relaxant and said the pain would subside. Kumi pleaded with her to keep me sedated in the hospital to get some rest but I told her I wanted to leave. The doctor prescribed a Valium tablet, which remains in my bag today. I was already confused and didn't want to add the unknown factor of a sedative. The chest pain eased.

The nights were impossible. I could not sleep; I could not stop crying. After everyone left and the night was quiet I tried to make sense of everything and failed. I had been run over and crushed by heavy equipment, that's how I describe my grief. I could not eat for the first five days after my son died. My body forgot how to do the normal things.

Every day leading up to Rikhado's funeral was filled with activity. I looked forward to the break of dawn because it meant there were things to do, places to go. I went to the Waterfall Legends Barbershop, Bianca and Rikhado's business, and admired the gorgeous flowers people placed outside to honour Rikhado, the wonderful messages and art they offered as a tribute to his life. Their offerings turned the shop into a beautiful shrine. I hung onto Val, Bianca's mum, in silent, uncontrollable emotion.

The key activity was cleansing the studio where Rikhado had died. Val's best friend Buyi is experienced in cleansing spaces and healing. The family gathered in a circle and shared prayers before we cleaned the studio and filled it with the fragrance of herbs, including lavender, that Buyi had brought. We smudged the whole space with incense.

When Rikhado's paternal grandmothers Koko Meims and Rakgadi arrived three days after his death I wished I could cuddle them and protect them from the pain. Both are in their nineties, but they made no fuss and maintained the calm presence of elders.

Bianca made arrangements for the funeral to take place at the Bryanston Catholic Church. We were under obligation to maintain COVID-19 protocols, therefore time and numbers in attendance were subject to restrictions. The funeral programme could only be an hour followed by a one-hour mass. The cremation was booked for 1pm so the programme had to be managed with precision to avoid delays. All the speakers were given no longer than five minutes, but some did not abide with that request. Kumi and I had to shorten our remarks and I did not read all of my short tribute. This is what I wanted to say at my son's funeral:

> My beloved son, Rikhado, MaRiky
>
> Between us there are no words that remain to be said. Words have become infinitely inadequate for us. Yesterday, as I rubbed your body with ancient embalming oils, it occurred to me as a blistering revelation that you are no longer this or that. YOU ARE EVERYTHING. You are no longer here or there. YOU ARE EVERYWHERE. In this reality, the significance of words as a communication tool diminishes tremendously.
>
> The inadequacy of words notwithstanding, I use them to address an uncontrollable desire. THE DESIRE TO GIVE THANKS. I give thanks for the mystery of your life. Preachers of some great sermons have characterised mystery not as that which is beyond knowing BUT that which can be known continuously. Since the day your spirit and body parted, facets of your life I previously had no appreciation for have been revealed to me. You established relationships for us in ways I would never have imagined. For this, I am thankful.
>
> I am thankful for the honour of being your mother. Even in the most troubled and disoriented periods of your life, your essential being still shone

through, and you honoured and loved people. For this I am deeply thankful.

I am thankful because you were a dedicated, loving partner to Bianca, your wife. The strong family ties you built between Bianca's family and ours are a treasured blessing and I give thanks for this. I give thanks and praise because you made your children Jordan and Maik the centre of your life. You loved them consistently and paved the path for us to continue raising them with love and respectful attention.

MaRiky, I am thankful because through your battling with the troubles of this world, including addiction, you taught me lasting lessons in equanimity. I learnt the grace of no judgement and openness to loving fully, even where choices made are at variance with those I preferred.

I will no longer see your beautiful, gentle eyes on your face, Mntanam, BUT I know I will see them in the early-morning chirping of the birds. The music of your voice I will now hear in the silence of the sleeping child, the winding roads, the valleys and the mountains. I will carry you in my heart and in all my being, every moment of my life. I LOVE YOU COMPLETELY. THE LORD GOD IS WITH YOU ALL THE TIME. FAREWELL MNTANAM, HAMBA KAHLE, VHAMSANDA, VHOMAKHADO.

It felt good to join family and friends for lunch after the service. To cope on that day I needed to be with people and to be busy. I was unable to deal with silence and contemplation. That night I watched Rikhado's videos and listened to his music.

I HAD BEEN TRAINING FOR A five-woman Mount Everest Base Camp expedition led by Jeanette McGill, a South African woman based in Australia. It was scheduled from 20 March to 4 April 2022. Xoli and I were joining the expedition that was postponed in 2020 because of the COVID-19 pandemic. When Nepal reopened the mountain I was excited about the prospect of finally going to Everest Base Camp. When Rikhado died I took the view that whatever will be, will be. After the funeral I wanted to go away into the far distance and engage with Rikhado there, so I decided I would join the expedition. Xoli and I were due to leave for Nepal on 19 March, Maik's birthday. When we landed in Kathmandu I checked my phone. My heart skipped a beat, there was an email from Rikhado. He had sent it less than 30 minutes before his last communication with Bianca. 'He wanted me to be on this trip,' I shouted with joy as I showed Xoli the email:

From: Rikhado Makhado <rikyrikyriky@gmail.com>
To: Louisa Zondo <lzondo>
Sent: Wednesday, 23 February 2022 at 02:54:09 GMT+2
Subject: I LOVE YOU

Be safe on your travels and thank you for being with us. I really enjoyed being around you Mama. Thank you for everything. I Love You SO MUCH.

Kind Regards
Rikhado "Riky Rick" Makhado

THE EUPHORIA OF BEING ON the mountain wore off immediately when we landed back at OR Tambo Airport. Everything was starting fresh and I did not have the tools to handle the disorientation of being in Rikhado's environment without him. I was angry and upset with everything. My bad mood affected Bianca and she had to talk to me about how unmanageable it was when she picked up my negative energy, because she relied on my energy to keep going. Within days of returning from Nepal I was harsh and closed towards Themba and Ntobeko. I apologised profusely to my family for being so inconsiderate. They were hurting as much as I was over the loss of Rikhado, and to ignore that was harmful. After spreading my negative energy at Bianca's home for two days after my return, I went to stay at Sheikani's home in an attempt to shake off my anger and bad mood.

I made an undertaking to remove myself from environments where I experienced a negative shift in mood, and to place myself in places of positive energy, like a brisk walk outside. Spending time with my grandchildren always energises me, so focusing on being present with them got me out of negative sentiment. I repaired my spirit and maintained a healthy relationship with my children.

I learned an enormous lesson about grief. Its multiple layers and nuances are not to be taken for granted. I thought I had shifted from acute grief while on the mountain but I had not, and grief overpowered me, presenting itself in cruel anger and hostility. We all need beams that keep focusing us on our emotions. Bianca, Themba and Ntobeko shone a beam of love that helped me to reclaim my joy. The pain never goes, it remains. Sometimes it overwhelms us and sometimes it co-exists with our lives.

At the start of South Africa's COVID-19 lockdown in March 2020, friends Nobantu Mpotulo and Nolitha Tsengiwe together with their fellow Buddhism teacher Moyra Keane, started a meditation community which sat together virtually every morning from 6am until 6.30am. I joined this sangha (a Sanskrit word denoting community and a fundamental of life in Buddhism) because I had embraced meditation as a calming, stabilising and grounding practice of opening my heart and calming my mind. An open and calm heart and mind strengthens the capacity for awareness, understanding and insight about my reactions, and cultivates the wisdom to approach everything, including my fears, with compassion. I was drawn to meditation practice in my search for methods to calm my unending tortured state. Body movement practices such as qigong and tai chi were also valuable in stimulating the opening of my heart. In the turmoil of the pandemic, the daily teachings on the nature of reality (dharma in Buddhism) followed by silent or guided meditation in our sangha helped me to navigate a path to peace.

I turned to the sangha as I grieved Rikhado's death. To my surprise, I discovered that sitting in silence flooded me with emotions which tore me up in the most terrifying ways. So I stopped sitting and started walking while I participated. After about four months, my capacity to sit through meditation gradually returned. Meditation practice remained a means of bringing calming awareness of my being and supported me in encountering my emotions with less fear.

My experience at church was similar. I could not join uManyano (the Methodist Women Prayer and Service Union) without shattering my broken heart. My church leaders and fellow Manyano members supported and held me in various ways, offering generous spiritual support and gentle caring and understanding throughout my inability to participate at church. I learnt that grief changes some things, fundamentally. I had to let go of all negative thoughts and emotion related to my inability to participate in uManyano while I grieved Rikhado's death. A year after Rikhado's death, I wrote to the chairperson of my Manyano structure to say that I might be ready to return to the women's union.

Rikhado's death caused me to feel that everything in my life was devoid of meaning and I harboured this belief for a long time. The truth presented itself in the many stories of people who suffered unbearable trauma and grief yet continued to live fully and purposefully. The widespread acknowledgement of the support and inspiration Rikhado was to many young people stirred me to commit to build on his legacy. I poured what limited energy I had into the establishment of the Riky Rick Foundation for the Promotion of Artivism to support young people in arts and culture through fellowship programmes. It also aims to: support initiatives in mental health and wellbeing; stimulate community building which strengthens people's sense of participation in their own destiny; and to energise the connection between the arts and culture and the achievement of desired social change (artivism). A year has passed since Rikhado's death and the foundation is about to be launched.

My heart breaks for the many who suffer to such an extent that they end their lives and for the many who suffer from the death of a loved one by suicide. I couldn't imagine what sadness and pain overcame my son until death presented itself as a better option. I was wracked by guilt, regret, sadness, anger and confusion about my contribution to his pain and depression (which he publicly spoke about) and my inability to do more to possibly avert his suicide. Shame over my own suicidal thoughts dominated my entire being until it drove me to seek help in therapy.

While I am deeply grateful that three-and-a-half months after Rikhado's death, Kumi and I went into therapy and have remained in therapy, I am troubled that many are unable to access even basic support to hold them through the dark journey that the soul takes when a loved one has died by suicide. The suicide rate in South Africa has reached epidemic proportions with 23.5 of every 100 000 people taking their own lives. With a suicide rate ranking ninth in the world and third on the African continent, there is every reason for mental health and wellbeing to be placed at the centre of all our endeavours. What would it take for the government, private sector, the non-profit sector and civil society to reimagine a country in which mental health services and the wellbeing of all is catered for?

Postscript:
We are not what has been done to us

Kumi and I had a five-hour, life-changing session with our therapist Dr D on 28 September. We began weekly therapy sessions in June 2022 to deal with the grief following Rikhado's death and explore rebuilding in our relationship. Dr D is an experienced transpersonal psychologist with a PhD in psychology. During his years of practice he has explored a range of methodologies and approaches, including indigenous and ancient wisdoms and traditions. His eclectic mix of skills made it easy for both of us to find resonance with him – not only as a psychotherapist but as a person we had met several years ago through our community work and participation in healing ceremonies.

My whole morning was filled with thoughts about the session scheduled from 10am to 3pm at Dr D's practice. I joined a meeting at 8am that Bianca had arranged with her attorney but I could not clear my mind and concentrate. Bianca wanted to confirm the date for the High Court to hear an application she brought, with the full support of the family, for an order requiring the High Court to issue her with letters of executorship. This would give her the right to handle matters relating to Rikhado's estate. They did not have a registered marriage even though they had a marriage relationship. The attorney confirmed that the matter was scheduled to come before the High Court on 10 October. Bianca was granted the order on that day.

As I walked towards Dr D's practice I realised that I was slightly early. Kumi, who was coming from Yeoville, had not yet arrived. I slowed down as I scanned my body for tension from the crown of my head to the soles of my feet. Each inhalation was a deep breath in and each exhalation a full breath out. I breathed until I released the tension and rested my body. Kumi arrived in good time for us to walk together into the practice.

Dr D welcomed us and invited us to sit on a mattress on the floor to keep us grounded while he explained the process. We had been in therapy for three-and-a-half months. As Kumi and I grieved together, and we both expressed a shared commitment to stay together for the rest of our lives and work on overcoming obstacles we encountered together. When we started therapy our relationship was threatened by my accumulation of debt; my persistent patterns of shutting Kumi out and being uncommunicative about everything; and the fact that I never had therapy following the attack at our home in February 1998 and never spoke to Kumi about it. We did not know whether we would be able to fulfil our commitment to be together.

Kumi and I attended three international gatherings together between May and June. At a psychedelic science conference in California, Kumi spoke about his recovery from the trauma of his sister's sudden death in 2018 and about the attack at our house. He said the two hours after the attackers had removed me from our bedroom were the longest two hours in his life. The second gathering was in Costa Rica that explored the possibilities of post-capitalist philanthropy. At a wellbeing summit in Bilbao, Spain, I presented my life as a case study in side-stepping healing processes and adversely affecting wellbeing. It was the first time I spoke in public about our attack.

Kumi said that as he listened to me speak, it struck him that I had absolutely no memory of what had happened during the attack. He was panic-stricken when he realised that he could not rely on my assertion that I had not been sexually assaulted. He had imagined the worst but hoped it had not happened. One of the attackers had covered my naked body with a sheet when I was in the bedroom as an act of kindness, so he had hoped that they had not carried out their threat to rape me and never doubted that I was telling the truth.

At our therapy sessions, Dr D facilitated a process of understanding how our childhoods had shaped us. The many rules I felt obliged to comply with in order to be valued and loved showed in the way I depleted and devalued myself in the hope that I would be loved. The tragic early loss of Kumi's mother cast him into a pattern of behaviour where he needed to take responsibility for everything to make life manageable and meaningful.

The therapy led us into exploring why we were together; what each of us wanted from life; what we needed from each other; and what we were able to commit to giving to each other. Our answers to these questions brought us closer together and we confirmed that we wanted to share all of our lives with each other. Our communication improved after we started therapy. Although we have addressed the bank debt, I have not yet disposed of the Kew house where we were attacked. My failure to address this or to embrace Kumi's offers to help had caused him much hurt, confusion and frustration. He was desperate to have the house and the debt out of our lives. Together with my unwillingness to seek therapy of any sort, this is what would leave us as best friends rather than partners for almost ten years. Both of us have grieved all that we had lost since the violent attack.

Kumi had asked Dr D at our first therapy session whether it was possible to surface a repressed memory. He said it was possible, but that it had to be done at the right time. After more than three months of therapy Dr D assessed our readiness to participate in memory work. The sessions had been gruelling for both of us. At times it surfaced extreme pain and unmanageable emotion and had brought us to the brink of giving up on everything. Dr D believed that we had developed strong foundations of trust and an understanding of who we were individually and in our relationship. He said he was willing to lead us into recovering memories of the attack if we were prepared. The five-hour session was scheduled for that work.

Dr D explained what he was going to do, offered each of us a capsule containing pharmaceutical grade MDMA, invited us to lie on our mattresses and led us through a deep-relaxation guided meditation. I felt extremely calm, the Eastern chants and songs soothed me. I had no idea how long I had been lying on the mattress before Kumi asked me what I was seeing. All my senses roared back into the Kew house. I felt those men pinning me down. They were suffocating and raping me. Kumi said I screamed so loud he was convinced I could be heard hundreds of metres away. Dr D and Kumi held onto my hands to prevent me from hurting myself. I cried a lot during that session. Kumi cried too as what he had suspected for twenty-five years was confirmed, and when he realised there were more men in the house than the two who had beaten him and tied him up in the bedroom.

We decided to tell the family the truth we had discovered about the attack. The following day, Kumi told the boys. After they cried, my sons told Kumi that the information explained so many things. They were referring to the instances when I would disconnect from all of them and close myself in the bedroom; the swings I made from complete disconnection from everyone to suddenly offering them unplanned, costly luxuries such as expensive shopping sprees and holidays overseas; or returning at the end of the day with a new car. They were beginning to make sense of the times when I was unexpectedly harsh towards them and the frantic state I would go into sometimes when they woke me up. I confided in Bianca. Kumi and I told Tandi and Jackie and we spoke to Naomi, who was in India. Following Dr D's advice to rely on water as a powerful cleansing element, that evening I filled the bathtub with hot water, added bath salts and soaked my body. I was numb but I wanted to feel my body, I did not want to abandon it. I wanted Kumi to be part of the cleansing so I called him to the bathroom and asked if he would bath me. We cried as he washed me, and it felt as though we were finally starting to heal from the brutality of twenty-five years earlier.

Healing is harder than I imagined anything could be. Kumi and I continue to work on healing our relationship. We both are developing the practice of finding our way back to each other to address hurts that we still cause on each other. We are getting better at communicating and addressing the causes of our conflicts and repairing the ruptures in our relationship as and when they happen. My body was not consistent, I still cannot fully trust and rely on it. It has a huge need for protection. But I am learning to free my body. When I told Dr D that I was struggling so much with being in my body that very often I felt as though it was impossible to continue, he recommended that I consult a bodywork specialist to free up my energy flow. Kumi and I now have additional support to release our bodies from the trauma and its effects. Through natural movements and sound we overcome the trauma reactions and gradually connect with the ease that recognises we are not what has been done to us.

My body may bear scars from twenty-five years ago and may, at times, react to them as though the trauma is happening now, but I am no longer trapped and stuck. I can move and escape from the trauma reaction to receive relief. The inconsistency of my body means that I still faint and fall to the ground when caught unawares by an overwhelming situation, or when triggered by a memory that has been recovered, but I am learning to slow down and cultivate my ability to be more aware, more times than not. In February I attended CottonFest and had an exhilarating time with family and friends. Kumi had asked whether I preferred to be at the festival or at home on my 59th birthday on 5 February, my first without Rikhado. I assumed that I would be at the festival because I enjoyed being with family. At midnight family and friends shared their birthday wishes; at the same time, the tribute to Rikhado began. As I took in the image of my son, I lost control of my body and fell on my back, knocking my head on the ground. I am learning from such incidents to pay attention to what my body is feeling so that I can offer the support it needs to keep functioning.

Many people have some idea of the devastating effect of rape and all forms of sexual assault and gender-based violence. As I joined the ranks of the millions who have experienced trauma and continued to navigate life to the best of their abilities, I committed myself to bringing compassion into all my interactions with the world. I equated this need to bring compassion into every interaction to the mantra: 'Leave a little space in your heart for the next person', which Rikhado loved, believed in and learnt from Dr Sam Motsuenyane, founder of African Bank.

As I continue my healing journey, I hold Rikhado's death as the event that gave me life. His death at the age of 34 gave me an opportunity to reclaim the essence of my life after losing it at the age of 34, when I was raped.

Acknowledgements

The process of writing this book was very challenging. For many months I seemed to lack the words to identify and express what I was experiencing. I am grateful to Kumi Naidoo, my beautiful love, for knowing how to be a supportive presence, devoid of pressure through the many months when words refused to surface, and grief made living with me a precarious balance.

Jacana Media went beyond the purview of a publisher's role and stood with me as a special family, absorbing my joys, concerns and deflation with care, and skilfully keeping me focused. I am deeply thankful to the Jacana team and the energising convening of Bridget Impey and Maggie Davey for all the guidance, support and advice you provided as this book came into existence.

Hagen Engler unlocked my voice and for that I cannot thank him enough. His calm interviewing style empowered me to pour out the stories without interruption from his presence. When I received the first set of transcribed pages beautifully organised by Hagen, I felt the shift, which started me writing, remembering, then being changed by the remembering.

Rehana Rossouw is precisely the editor I needed for this work. Maintaining the stance of an unfazed doula – all prepared to encounter the unknown as it presents itself – Rehana brought a sense of stability into my frenetic attempts to meet very tight deadlines. I am thankful for her insightful editing.

I am deeply grateful to the Community Arts Lab for the fellowship that enabled me to pursue this writing, the Barloworld Empowerment Foundation for always encouraging and supporting me, and the Community Arts Network for exposing me to highly stimulating engagements on the place of arts and culture in the story of the universe.

My friends and spiritual community deserve a special word of gratitude because without them even knowing their impact they have always helped me to navigate the challenges of life. Xoli, Penny and Nomfanelo responded positively to a desperate request I made to them in June 2022, when all of life seemed to be caving in on me. I asked them to be by my side as soul sisters, absorbing everything with me, and without knowing what this would mean, they agreed. Since that time, they have carried me and my burden with enormous grace and generosity. I bow to you.

I am thankful to my entire family for touching me with love. Your existence gives special meaning to life. Lastly, how do I give thanks to life? Perhaps I can do that by wanting to give thanks to and honour all facets of life itself.

Photo captions

Page i

Top left: My parents' wedding day, 16 December 1958, in Mnceba, Tabankulu in the Eastern Cape Province

Top right: As a nurse at McCord Hospital, my mother looks pretty.

Middle left: 1979 school holidays, sitting outside our house at B986 KwaMashu

Middle right: In 1977 my mother joined my father on a trip to the USA. This was her first international trip.

Bottom left: 1979 school holidays, posing at B986 next to the only tree we had in our yard – a lemon tree (not to be confused with the tall tree in our neighbour's yard)

Bottom right: 1979 Inanda Seminary, posing on the school grounds, the village in the background

Page ii

Top left: December 1983 carrying my first-born son, Sheikani. He is six months old.

Top right: Portugal 1987, visiting my sister who was posted in Portugal as a South African diplomat. I am sitting with my mother in this photo.

Bottom left: Portugal 1987: My sister and her children
From left to right: Tebogo Sililo, Monaheng Sililo, Tandi Zondo and Lebogang Sililo

Bottom right: 27 July 1988, celebrating Rikhado's first birthday at my mother's house, D1664 KwaMashu. I'm behind the birthday boy. My sister, Tandi, stands next to me carrying her first-born daughter, Tebogo Sililo. Rikhado's older brother, Sheikani, wearing a denim jacket, is seated next to his best friend, Andile "MaA".

Page iii

Top left: January 1998, on holiday for my first visit to Cape Town. Rikhado turned six months old and started his first baby conversations during this trip.

Top right: London 1988, this photo was taken after a meeting of the Association of South African Students (ASAS). South African students from various parts of the UK gathered on this day. I am seated on the lowest step.

Middle: This photo was taken during a visit to Berlin in October 1989. The wall was still intact.

Bottom left: Edinburgh 1989, at the launch of the Association of South African Students (ASAS). Pinned on the wall behind me is a painting depicting an artist's impression of what Mandela looked like at that point, 25 years out of sight in incarceration.

Bottom right: Berlin 1989, after writing my Master of Laws examinations at the London School of Economics, I bought a one month's pass for travel through Europe and started my tour in Germany. In this photo we are pushing the car through gridlocked traffic on the Autobahn. In that heavy traffic, we were better off pushing the car than trying to drive it.

Page iv

Top left: Germany 1989, walking through the woods in Darmstadt with my best friend, Xoli Kakana

Top right: London School of Economics days, celebrating Africa Day, 25 May 1989, with lovely friends

From left to right: Me, Lulu Gwagwa and Naomi Nontombi Tutu

Bottom left: Canada 1990, during an International Human Rights Programme. Prof. Humphrey, public international law expert and Mrs Humphrey are the elders in the photo. Wendy Singh (Barbados) and I stand on the ends of the photo. Next to me stands a colleague from Myanmar. A colleague from Peru stands between Prof. and Mrs Humphrey.

Bottom right: Frankfurt Airport 1990, on a visit to Germany where Xoli was living and studying

From left to right: Veli Tshabalala, myself, Luyanda and Xoli Kakana

Page v

Top left: In September 1992 our family had a Thanksgiving ceremony. The after party was held at the home of Ray Zondo, now Chief Justice of South Africa.

Top right: Toasting at the 1992 family Thanksgiving ceremony

From left to right: Uncle R.S. Canca (my mother's cousin), Aunt Nomayeza Canca, FN Zondo (my mother), Enid Bolani (my mother's best friend), Mrs Zondo (my uncle Windam's wife) and Paul Zondo (uncle)

Middle: Celebrating my mother's 70th birthday, 30 October 2000. My mother, in the centre, is flanked by the most important women in her life: on her left is Mrs Nomsa Jessie Magore (née Mayeza), her cousin, and Mrs Enid Bolani is on her right.

Bottom left: Yaounde, Cameroon, May 1996, attending the international conference on national human rights institutions

From left to right: Barney Pityana (Chairperson of the South African Human Rights Commission), Selby Bhaqwa (Public Protector), me, Shirley Mabusela (Deputy Chairperson of the South African Human Rights Commission)

Bottom right: This photo was taken in 1996, during my term as a Deputy Executive Director of the Constitutional Assembly (AC) Secretariat. To my right is the Executive Director of the CA, Hassen Ebrahim with a foreign mission delegation.

Page vi

Top left: Aggra, India, January 2004, Kumi and me at the Taj Mahal complex on the margins of the 2004 World Social Forum held in Mumbai

Top right: Mumbai 2004, a photo taken after a generous invitation from Husein to join his family for lunch at his home. Kumi and I met Husein at a local cellphone shop. In addition to enjoying a delicious vegetarian meal, we also learnt a lot about not burdening the body by eating more than a handful of solid food and filling the rest of the stomach space with water.

From left to right: Husein, his mother, his sister and me, with the family's neighbour in the background

Bottom left: Christmas Day 2011

Seated from left to right: My son Themba Mdladla, me, my sisters Tandi Zondo and Jackie Zondo

Standing from left to right: My sons Ntobeko Mdladla and Rikhado Makhado, my nephews Monaheng Sililo and Nkululeko Zondo, and my nieces Tebogo Sililo and Aphiwe Gumede

Bottom right: With my four sons on my eldest son Sheikani's wedding day in 2011

From left to right: Rikhado Makhado, me, Sheikani Makhado, Themba Mdladla and Ntobeko Mdladla

Page vii

Top left: 18 July 2018, taking a breath at Stella Point before walking the longest 170 metres to summit at Uhuru an hour later

Top right: 2018, Naomi Alexander-Naidoo – the doting aunt to my grandchildren – here she has Maik on her lap.

Bottom left: Rikhado, Bianca and the children on holiday with Bianca's parents
   From left to right: Rikhado Makhado, his wife Bianca Naidoo, my granddaughter Jordan Plaatjes, Bianca's parents Valerie Pillay and Morgan Pillay and my grandson Maik Makhado

Bottom right: Sheikani and 'MaA': the age difference did not stand in the way of these two being best friends and roaming the neighbourhood from dawn to dusk. Sheikani is five and 'MaA' is three years old.

Page viii

Top left: From left to right: my sister Jackie Zondo, my niece Aphiwe Gumede and my nephew Fez Zondo

Top right: My oldest son and his children
   From left to right: Mia Makhado, Sheikani Makhado and Kaya Makhado

Bottom left: My oldest sister Tandi and her children
   From left to right: Nkululeko Zondo, Tebogo Sililo, Monaheng Sililo, Lebogang Sililo and Tandi Zondo

Bottom right: Turning 59, celebrating with Sheikani's children
   From left to right: Kaya Makhado (turning five on 11 June 2023), me, and Mia Makhado (turning ten on 22 October 2023)